Strategic Defamation of Fethullah Gülen

English vs. Turkish

Doğan Koç

UNIVERSITY PRESS OF AMERICA,® INC.

Lanham · Boulder · New York · Toronto · Plymouth, UK

Copyright © 2012 by
University Press of America,® Inc.
4501 Forbes Boulevard
Suite 200
Lanham, Maryland 20706
UPA Acquisitions Department (301) 459-3366

10 Thornbury Road
Plymouth PL6 7PP
United Kingdom

Library of Congress Control Number: 2012938539
ISBN: 978-0-7618-5930-7 (paperback : alk. paper)
eISBN: 978-0-7618-5931-4

Contents

Chapter I

Introduction

In recent years, Fethullah Gülen and the Hizmet (service) Movement have attracted significant attention from both Western and Muslim populations. Academic conferences in Houston, London, Washington, Amsterdam, Berlin, Cairo, Cape Town, Los Angeles, Delhi, and Jakarta, have analyzed the growth and influence of the movement. Gülen himself has been the topic of hundreds of articles and books, and leading newspapers around the world have reported on the Hizmet Movement. The French newspaper "Le Monde" analyzed the Hizmet Movement schools inspired by Fethullah Gülen in Germany, suggesting that they could provide an example to the French immigrant population (Borne 2008). The New York Times also featured a cover story on the Hizmet Movement schools in Pakistan, this time pointing them as a possible remedy for the spread of radical Islam (Tavernise 2008).

With this growing public awareness has come increased critical attention. New scholarly research has resulted in several masters and PhD theses investigating topics related to the movement, and critical reflection on the teachings of Fethullah Gülen and the activities of the Hizmet Movement is essential for the movement's continued relevance. While Gülen's efforts for education and dialogue are typically applauded by politicians and government officials, the formulation of various critiques by researchers and scholars is to be expected and welcomed as a sign of the very cultural dialogue that Gülen works to promote. However, among a small group of authors, criticism has given way to flagrant defamation. Here the term "defamation" is not used frivolously; it denotes the deliberately slanderous or libelous injury of another's good reputation. Such injury obviously offends the many educators and social workers who identify themselves with Fetullah Gülen, but it also precludes the possibility of honest and unguarded critical dialogue between the Hizmet Movement and its social neighbors in both Western and Muslim countries.

This book offers a comprehensive analysis of the vilification of Fethullah Gülen at work in both English and Turkish texts in order to illustrate that these defamatory articles and books do not offer any consistent critique; they are consistent only with the fears of their intended audiences. As Türker (2009) has demonstrated, a fundamental inconsistency exists between the defamatory picture of Gülen that appears in Turkish and the defamatory picture of him that appears in English. In the Muslim world, Gülen is depicted as a Zionist CIA agent, a US puppet, or even a secret cardinal of the Pope. Articles warn that he is a Western Trojan horse, trying to either Christianize Muslims or allow for the Western exploitation of the Muslim world. On the other hand, English articles depict Gülen as a nefarious anti-Semitic or anti-Western presence, whose moderate Islam is a secret plot to Islamize Christians. Here, defamatory authors warn that he is an Islamist Trojan horse: a second Khomeini trying to establish an Islamic caliphate in the world. And Türker is cynical of such directly contradictory warnings:

> It makes more sense to warn Turkish speakers of an American imperialist danger that is supported by Zionists. But on the other hand, for English speakers, you will find more buyers if you use an Islamic danger argument.

To take a brief example, Hikmet Cetinkaya appears to calculate in precisely this way. In Turkish, he has authored ten books and several articles claiming that Fetullah Gülen is a puppet of US political interests, whose religious message conceals a subversive secularism masterminded by the American government (see "Defamation of Gülen in Turkish" and "Appendix" for more information). However, when the same Hikmet Cetinkaya appears on a Dutch documentary, he warns the Dutch people that Gülen leads a dangerous radical religious movement whose progressive social actions conceal a secret Islamist agenda (Sharon-Krespin 2009). In other words, when he addresses a Turkish audience, Hikmet Cetinkaya typically portrays Gülen as an American puppet. But when he addresses a Western audience, Gülen is portrayed as an Islamic danger to the West. The contradictory accusations of Hikmet Cetinkaya could perhaps be dismissed as an isolated case of distortion, but unfortunately he is not alone in making such defamatory statements. And as this book hopes to demonstrate, when the sum total of defamatory articles written in either English or Turkish is analyzed as a whole, this very same inconsistency appears.

This book shows that Hikmet Cetinkaya is not alone in these defamation 'campaigns,' there is a wide group of people who act strategically when defaming Fethullah Gülen and the Hizmet Movement.

Chapter 2

Fethullah Gülen and the Hizmet Movement

2.1. BIOGRAPHY OF FETHULLAH GÜLEN

Before examining the various defamatory articles and books, it is necessary to understand a little bit about Fethullah Gülen and the Hizmet Movement. Fethullah Gülen is a moderate Turkish Muslim scholar, known primarily as an advocate of education and religious dialogue. He began his career as a preacher and an education activist, and his ideas have mobilized millions of people towards civic engagement. This "Hizmet Movement," sometimes referred to as the Gülen Movement, denotes the unofficial affiliation of those who are committed to Gülen's vision of education, dialogue, peace, social justice, and social harmony. The popularity of Gülen's teachings and the dedication of the Hizmet Movement have resulted in the establishment of hundreds of education and dialogue institutions throughout the world.

M. Fethullah Gülen was born in 1941 in the town of Erzurum, located in the eastern part of Turkey (Erdogan, 1995). His father was an imam and a farmer, and Fethullah Gülen was the second eldest in a family of seven children. He received a traditional education from both family members and religious institutions, and initiated the rigorous regimen of self-education that he would continue throughout his life. Gülen explains these early encounters with education:

> My first teacher was my mother. At that time, our village had no elementary school. Later, one was opened. My first Arabic and Persian teacher was my father. Later, I was taught by Muhammed Lutfi Efendi's grandson, Sadi Efendi. While studying the religious sciences, I also read other books and studied the Sufi sciences. For me, traces of the religious sciences and Sufism always produced the same rhythm (Erdogan, p.35).

Despite a lack of formal education, the depth of Gülen's knowledge in various traditions has surprised several of his biographers. In his analysis of Gülen's educational life, Tuncer (2005) admires his comprehensive knowledge of not only traditional Islamic sources, but Western, Eastern, Turkish, and modern Islamic sources as well. Gülen's self-education began when he read the Qur'an at age three, later committing it to memory (Tuncer 2005). Aras & Caha (2000) also cite Gülen's extensive knowledge of both traditional Islamic sources and Western philosophy, emphasizing his interest in the work of Immanuel Kant.

At the age of fourteen, Gülen began preaching in local mosques. In 1959, he passed a state exam and left Erzurum for Edirne, where he would become a state preacher at the Ucserefeli Mosque. By August 6, 1959, Gülen had been officially appointed the imam second in charge. He served for three years in Edirne, and then traveled to Kestanepazari, Izmir, Turkey's third largest city. Gülen's years in Izmir are considered to be the founding years of his community. His service here in the field of education, beginning with the Kestanepazari Qur'anic School and continuing through his travels as a preacher throughout Western Anatolia, gained him popularity in the late 1960s and early 1970s. Gülen explains these pivotal years:

> At Kestanepazari [Izmir], I was busy with students. My official duty was not limited to Izmir, for I was expected to travel in the Aegean part of Turkey. From time to time I would go to coffeehouses to explain things to the men who were killing time there. (Erdogan, 1995, p.53)

During this time, a small community of students and laypeople began to take shape with Gülen at its center. According to his interview with Erdogan (1995), he was spending most of his time in Izmir preaching, giving conferences, studying, and teaching.

Gülen was then appointed to Edremit, to Manisa, and finally to Bornova, Izmir, where he worked until September 12, 1980. As he continued to travel, Gülen's popularity increased. His discourse was distinguished for its depth of knowledge, sensitivity, and eloquence, and audiences all over the country gathered to hear him address various religious, social, economic, and philosophical issues. His sermons were highly structured, and his systematic presentation of a topic might extend over many months, an uncommon practice at that time.

Gülen's teachings attracted the attention of the academic community and common people alike. Traveling to numerous cities and towns across Turkey, he would give sermons in mosques and then give public speeches in theatres and coffee houses. These sermons and speeches were often recorded on tape, and volunteers all around the country distributed such tapes, further amplifying his influence. Although he was only in his thirties, Gülen had already become one of the few preachers to achieve such nationwide recognition.

After his retirement in 1981, Gülen continued to give speeches and sermons into the early 1990s.

Aside from his reputation as an orator, Gülen continued to attract significant media attention due to his educational activities and support for religious dialogue. In the late 1990s, Gülen was interviewed by several different media organizations, and these televised appearances helped introduce him to a much wider population. Gülen's personality also helped him to gain fame in intellectual circles, as his books have become bestsellers in Turkey (Aras & Caha, 2000). As Nuriye Akman, a senior Turkish columnist, states:

> He is like that "old-style gentleman" we read about in old books and see in old films. He says *"estagfurullah"* [I beg the pardon of God] in every other sentence. He speaks in delicate and polite phrases. He is extremely modest.... He speaks in an even tone knowing what he will say and uses correct grammar and an Ottoman vocabulary. (Akman 1995, p.16-18)

Dale F. Eickelman, an American expert on Islam and Middle East, speaks of Gülen as Turkey's answer to Billy Graham, the media-savvy American evangelist. In televised chat shows, interviews, and occasional sermons, Gülen speaks about Islam and science, democracy, modernity, religious and ideological tolerance, the importance of education, and various current events (Eickelman 1998).

Although some people remain suspicious of his influence, Gülen has generally gained the support of civil and political leaders in Turkey.[1] He has visited with political leaders from both left and right wing parties and has met with Jewish and Christian leaders, even Pope John II, at varoius interfaith dialogue events. In 1999, Gülen moved to United States for medical treatment, where he still lives today.

Gülen continues to write in an almost cloistral life while teaching Islamic sciences to a small number of students. In addition to his books, Gülen contributes editorials to *Sizinti, Yeni Ümit, Yagmur,* and *The Fountain* magazines. His sermons and discourses have been recorded on thousands of tapes and video cassettes, and many books have been compiled from these sources. Currently, he communicates with the world and with the Hizmet Movement through his writings published in magazines and on the internet.

2.2. HISTORY OF THE HIZMET MOVEMENT

Althouh he began teaching at the Kestanepazari Qur'anic School in 1966, people did not start to organize around Gülen's ideas until the 1970s (Hermansen, 2005). Inspired by his emphasis on education, the first study center (*dersane*) was established by people around Gülen in 1978 to prepare high school students for the nationwide university entrance examination.[2] Currently, there are hundreds of *dersanes* all over Turkey, and every year; these centers generate the top test scores. In 1979, the movement began to publish the journal *Sizinti*, promoting a synthesis of scientific knowledge and Islam (Agai, 2005).

After the 1980 military coup, legal changes enabled the opening of state-controlled private schools. Gülen then encouraged people around him to open private secular schools that would include English as a primary language and put more emphasis on science. After the collapse of Soviet Union, similar schools were opened in the Central Asian Turkic countries. Now, there are over one thousand schools inspired by Gülen's ideas in more than a hundred different countries (Ebaugh 2009).

The Hizmet Movement has established a sizeable media network, including a newspaper (Zaman), a televison station (STV), several radio stations, an academic theology magazine (Yeni Umit), a literature magazine (Yagmur), an ecology magazine (Ekoloji), a news magazine (Aksiyon), and a news agency (Cihan Haber Ajansi).[3] According to Aras & Caha (2000) the movement draws much of its support from young urban men, with a special appeal to doctors, academics, and other professionals. Hakan Yavuz explains the intentions of those who identify themselves with the teachings of Gülen in an interview with *Religioscope* conducted in 2004:

> The movement is very active, responsible for newspapers, financial institutions, the best hospitals and private high schools in Turkey, and so forth. It is part of every aspect of Turkish life. It tries to set a good example and to improve standards. I think it is well integrated into Turkish society.
>
> The movement wants to provide a good image of Islam, not so much through indoctrination, but to teach Islam through its members setting a good example by becoming good doctors, good mathematicians, good politicians, good cooks, and so forth. Such people want to teach Islam by doing their duty properly.
>
> In a way, they represent a new model of Islam in Turkey, at peace with democracy and modernity. This also reflects the Anatolian understanding of Islam, i.e. the Sufi conception of morality is at the centre of the movement (Religioscope, 2004, interview with Hakan Yavuz).

The Hizmet Movement is ultimately an array of service projects initiated, funded, and conducted by people who are motivated to various extents by Gülen's humanitarian discourse. In a surprisingly short time, the movement has become active in over a hundred countries, with an extensive education and media network that spans Turkey, Central Asia, the Balkans, Southeast Asia, West Africa, Russia, Mongolia, China, Australia, Western Europe, and the United States (Hendrick, 2006).

In order to understand the Hizmet Movement and its development, it is necessary to examine the beliefs and motivations of its participants. Since these beliefas are often directly influenced by the teachings of Fethullah Gülen, the Hizmet Movement is often characterized as a unique amalgamation of civic engagement and religious identity. Aras and Caha (2000) define the movement as simultaneously Islamic, liberal, and modern, whereas Yavuz (2003) prefers to discuss it as a set of contemporary and ultimately pragmatic reforms. But the movement's ability to reconcile traditional Islamic values with modern life and science is its most characteristic feature, and this is precisely what has enabled Gülen to gather such a large, receptive audience (Aras and Caha 2000).

2.2.1. Islam

The movement must first be approached in terms of its Islamic identity. Fethullah Gülen is first and foremost a prominent religious leader in Turkey, and he regularly uses Islamic sources to motivate and mobilize the people around him. Thus, a comprehension of Gülen's particular interpretation of Islam will be essential to the understanding of the movement and its activities.

For Yavuz (2004), the Hizmet Movement represents a model of Islam that is at peace with democracy and modernity, typifying the Anatolian understanding of religion and morality. Researchers[4] who have studied the movement agree that it mobilizes a particularly Sufi conception of morality. Even though Gülen does not establish a Sufi order in its common sense[5], he does seek to recontextualize basic principles of the Sufi life within a modern framework (Gokcek 2005). Gülen is often portrayed as the leader of a "social movement" encouraging a private morality modeled after Sufism rather than a traditional Sufi tariqa[6] (Williams 2005; Yavuz 2004). This relationship to the Sufi tradition has led some scholars to refer to the Hizmet Movement as "quasi-Sufi," "Sufi-oriented," or even "post-Sufism" (Kim 2005; Yavuz 2004).

To cut a long story short, Sufism denotes the personal, spiritual aspect of Islam: the inner life of a practicing Muslim (Chittick, 1999). In Gülen's own definition, Sufism is a life-long process of spiritual development that demands the individual's active participation. Strict observance of all religious obligations and adherence to the Prophet Muhammad's example are meant to enable individuals, through the practice of constant worship, to deepen their awareness of themselves as devotees of God (Gülen, 1999). The Qur'an and Sunnah (tradition of the Prophet Muhammed) are the foundations of this practice (Yavuz, 2004). Gülen summarizes his understanding of Sufism as follows:

> Sufism is the path followed by an individual who, having been able to free himself or herself from human vices and weakness in order to acquire angelic

qualities and conduct that pleases God, lives in accordance with the requirements of God's knowledge and love and in the resulting spiritual delight that
ensues (Gülen, 1999, p.xiv).

Although he praises Sufism (tasawwuf), Gülen refuses the title of Sufi
Sheikh and denies that the Hizmet Movement is in any way a Sufi *tariqah*[7]
(Özkök, 1995). In this way, Gülen's understanding of Sufism resembles that
of the early centuries of Islam. His practice calls to mind the first and second
centuries of Islam, before Sufism had been institutionalized. Sarioprak (2001)
calls Gülen "a Sufi in his own way," pointing to parallels between Gülen's
insistence that he is not the leader of a religious movement and the attitude
of early Sufi scholars:

> Early Sufis had neither orders nor even Sufi organizations. Rabia, Junayd,
> Muhasibi, Bishr, Ghazzali, Feriduddin Attar, and even Rumi did not belong to
> a tariqah. However they were Sufis.

This Sufi understanding with a typically Ottoman-Turkish[8] approach to
Islam has shaped Gülen's characteristic interpretation of the role of religion
in public life (Aras & Caha, 2000). He interprets most Islamic regulations as
applying to an individual's private life, with only a small portion of them con-
cerning the role of government. And according to Gülen, these latter provi-
sions need not be enforced. Religion is a private matter, and its requirements
should not be imposed on anyone (Gülen, 1995). Aras and Caha (2000) emphasize the influence of Anatolian history and culture on this interpretation
of Islam. According to Aras and Caha (2000), the movement's interpretation
of Islam is liberal and tolerant of non-Islamic lifestyles, which is rooted again
in Anatolian historical experience and Sufi traditions. All creatures are to be
loved as reflections of God and objects of His own love, leaving no place for
enemies or "others" (Gülen, 2004).

2.2.2. Education

The Hizmet Movement is primarily known for the network of schools it
has created around the world. Among those inspired by Gülen, education is
regarded as the pivotal field of service. Yavuz (2004) asserts that work of
education is at the very core of the Hizmet movement's identity, which he refers to not as a religious movement, but rather an education-oriented and one.
As mentioned previously, the movement entered the educational field first in
1978 by establishing private university preparatory centers. After the 1980
military coup made possible the establishment of private schools, the Private

Yamanlar High School in Izmir and Private Fatih High School in Istanbul became the movement's first high schools, opened in 1982.[9] The subsequent success of graduates from these schools and private centers has brought the Hizmet Movement widespread public recognition.[10] And after the dissolution of Soviet Union, the movement started to open exceptional high schools in former Soviet Union countries, and then all over the world.

Throughout his public life, Gülen taught that learning is the main duty and obligation of all humans:

> The main duty and purpose of human life is to seek understanding. The effort of doing so, known as education, is a perfecting process through which we earn, in the spiritual, intellectual, and physical dimensions of our beings, the rank appointed for us as the perfect pattern of creation (Unal and Williams, 2000, p.305).

For Gülen, education is a defining human characteristic that distinguishes us from other creatures:

> We are truly human if we learn, teach, and inspire others. It is difficult to regard those who are ignorant and without desire to learn as truly human. (Unal and Williams, 2000, p.309)

When he discusses education, Gülen typically emphasizes the importance of both individual and societal change. Education is for him the essence of humanity, but it also sustains a well-balanced society. Thomas Michel (2003), who has studied various Gülen-inspired schools around the world, claims that Gülen's educational understanding reflects Turkey's particular educational dilemma. In a sense, Gülen's educational project can be read as an attempt to combine the strengths of each school. He envisions a "marriage of hearts and minds" that would provide instruction in science, reason, and morality and mold individuals of "thought, action, and inspiration" (Gülen, 1996).

The schools established by the movement provide a secular education with an emphasis on the sciences.[11] Each institution is run independently, although each shares a common vision, sometimes even a common curriculum (Williams, 2005). The balance of instruction in science, reason, and morality envisioned by Gülen is achieved by providing students with a high quality education and exemplary teachers. None of the schools offer religious education. Instead, the teachers model moral and ethical behavior in their daily life. Today, an enormous diversity of ethnic groups are a part of the same community, and the teachers of the Hizmet Movement insist that this shared experience must be accompanied by shared understanding and a shared code of ethics. It is this "universal" code of ethics that the schools hope to convey. Hizmet Movement schools employ all kinds of teachers: Turkish, non-Turkish, Muslim, and non-Muslim. And according to Agai (2005), many of the students at such schools have never heard the name "Fethullah Gülen." In this sense it would be a mistake to call the schools "Gülen schools" as many casually do. But on the other hand, without Gülen's inspiration it is almost certain that such schools would not exist.

2.2.3. Dialogue

Aside from education, the most characteristic activity of the Hizmet Movement is the promotion of interfaith dialogue and tolerance.[12] Gülen emphasizes the importance of tolerance and dialogue in his teachings, and these values have become central to the Hizmet Movement's mission and identity (Hendrick, 2005).

> Among the many things we have lost, perhaps the first and most important is tolerance. From this word we understand embracing people regardless of difference of opinion, world-view, ideology, ethnicity, or belief. It also means putting up with matters we do not like by finding strength in a deep conscience, faith and a generous heart or by strength of our emotions. From another approach, it means, in the words of the famous Turkish poet Yunus[13], loving the created simply because of the Creator (Gülen 2004a. p.46).

In his writings, speeches, sermons, and interviews, Gülen praises the person who practices dialogue, tolerance, and love:

> Throughout the four corners of the world, people of truth and love, by acting on these truths, are carrying messages of love, tolerance, and dialogue with everyone (Gülen, 2004b, p.174).

Gülen considers dialogue and tolerance to be the two essential pillars of a peaceful, democratic society. "Dialogue" he defines as the coming together of two or more people for the sake of discussion and community. Such dialogue requires a patient tolerance that accepts others and is willing to learn how to get along with them as they are. Gülen argues that this conception of tolerance is clearly grounded in Islamic texts, and emphasizes that tolerance does not require a person to forego his or her own traditions or beliefs (Gülen, 2004b).

Aslan (2005) situates Gülen's approach to dialogue in the Islamic tradition, arguing that he deploys the Qur'an, Sunnah, and the intellectual tradition of Sufism in order to establish a clear precedent within Islam for cultural coexistence. According to Gülen, interfaith dialogue is not alien to Islam; it is the natural result of the practice of Islamic ethics. Aras & Caha (2000) suggest that this project is not new. Gülen's conception of dialogue is rooted in the Anatolian experience of Islam. Gülen himself support this view and talks about this as "Turkish Muslimness" (Gülen, 2004b ; Unal and Williams, 2000, p.56). He emphasizes the universality of Islam, but often favors an interpretation of it closely associated with the historical practice of Muslim Turks rooted in Central Asia and Anatolia.

As an advocate of dialogue, Gülen has met with various Christian and Jewish religious leaders, including Patriarch Bartholomeos, head of the Greek Orthodox Fener Patriarchate in Istanbul. In February 1998, he visited Pope John Paul II in Rome and received a visit from Israel's Sephardic Head Rabbi Eliyahu Bakshi Doron. In Turkey, the Hizmet Movement has established the Journalists' and Writers' Foundation, which brings intellectuals together across the ideological spectrum to promote discussion. Numerous institutions for dialogue have been established by Gülen-inspired people around the world. These initiatives aim to bring their respective communities together in order to promote understanding, mutual respect, compassion, and broader community service.

2.2.4. Science and Modernity

Another common point of emphasis in Gülen's teachings is the importance of science and modernity. According to him, a good Muslim needs to catch up with the modern developments and also needs to obey the scientific laws as much as divine laws:

> So, Muslims must realize both intellectual and spiritual enlightenment. The light of the intellect is scientific knowledge while the heart or spirit derives its light from religious science. Scientific knowledge without religion usually causes atheism or agnosticism while religious knowledge without intellectual enlightenment gives rise to bigotry. When combined, they urge a student to further and further research and deepening in both belief and knowledge (Gülen, 1997, p.320).

Gülen does not see any conflict between science and religion; they are both regulations established by God. Gülen requires science and knowledge for the development and illumination of mind, whereas he underlines the path to misguidance and deception in the absence of both (Gülen, 2000). According to Gülen, scientific knowledge is a universal product, having developed over time according to the contributions of many civilizations. Although Muslims have played an important role in this evolution, Western nations have led the world in innovation for last three centuries. But this should not suggest an incompatibility between science and non-Western culture. He regrets the lack of scientific involvement in the Muslim world today and encourages Muslims to engage with and transform and the contemporary field. If the twentieth century was an era of science, the twenty-first will be even more so (Gülen, 2000).

Gülen argues that man lives in an age of science and technology for which there is no alternative. Instead of resisting it, he seeks to articulate a "middle way between modernity and the Muslim tradition" (Kuru 2003). According to Kuru's analysis, Gülen does not invent a "middle way" between modernity and Islam, for he sees Islam itself as this middle way. For Gülen, Islam is the balance between materialism and spirituality, between rationalism and mysticism, between worldliness and asceticism, between this world and next (Gülen 1995). He calls Muslims to *"sirat-i mustakim"* (the straight path) and to be "ummeten vasatan" (community of the middle way).[14] According to Michel (2005), Gülen criticizes both the traditional schools (madrasas, takyas) and the modern, secular state and military academies. Gülen critiques the former for a lack of scientific knowledge, and the latter for a lack of spiritual and ethical values:

> In both cases, that of the madrasas and takyas and that of the state schools and military academies, the root problem is the same, the lack of integration- integration of the new and the old, of modernity and tradition, of scientific and religious knowledge, of ethical skills and character formation. The result of this lack of integration is a society in crisis (Michel 2005).

Gülen argues that modernity and modernism are not the same, and he criticizes the modernism whose ultimate goal is simply modernity. Instead, he suggests that a richer concept of "civilization" should be the true goal of nations:

> Modern facilities can help to 'modernize' the outward appearance of life, but that does not amount to being civilized... [Civilization] is a final destination reached along a rational way going through time and circumstances. Civilization is different from modernism. While the former means the changing and renewal of man with respect to his views, way of thinking and human aspects, the latter consists in the changing of life-style and bodily pleasures and the development of living facilities (Gülen 1998).

In Turkey's political context, Yavuz (2004) defines Gülen's ideal modernity as "bottom-up modernity": one that is internalized by the masses rather than imposed by the state.

2.2.5. Politics

As mentioned above, Gülen teaches that most Islamic regulations pertain to the private lives of individuals. Only a small few deal directly with matters of the state and government, and these can be easily practiced within the framework of democracy (Sabah, 1995, and Aras & Caha, 2000). In other words, only a small portion of the teachings of Islam concern political life, and they are in no way incompatible with modern democracy. Gülen states:

> Islam does not propose a certain unchangeable form of government or attempt to shape it. Instead, Islam establishes fundamental principles that orient a government's general character, leaving it to the people to choose the type and form of government according to time and circumstances. If we approach the matter in this light and compare Islam with today's modern liberal democracy, we will better understand the position of Islam and democracy with respect to each other (Gülen 2001, p.134).

He believes that the democratic form of government is the best choice for modern nations. But nonetheless, democracy has evolved over time and will continue to develop in the future. Gülen criticizes the regimes in Iran and Saudi Arabia and emphasizes the historical compatibility of Islam and democracy by making frequent reference to the life of Prophet and the first four caliphs of Islam (Aras & Caha, 2000).

According to Yavuz (2004), Gülen wants religion to remain above politics, opposing the unification of church and state for fear that politics would corrupt religion. In his analysis of top-bottom, and bottom-up conceptions of modernity, Yavuz (2004) also points out the practice of secularism in Turkey is not synonymous with this separation of religion and politics. Rather, "secularism" has come to define the identity of the ruling elite that has generated major reactions from the Anatolian masses. In the top-down modernity practiced by the Turkish state, secularism takes the form of French *laïcisme*; it leaves no room for religion in public sphere and tries to cleanse the public domain of all religious expression (Yavuz 2004). However, the bottom-up modernity approaches secularism in the historically Anglo-Saxon way: it acknowledges religion as a source of morality and ethics but defends the separation of religion and politics. Yavuz (2004) sees Gülen as a representative of this bottom-up Turkish modernity and an advocate for its realization.

Saribay (1995) supports Gülen's reading of Islam as a religion compatible with human rights and democratic modernity. In this sense, the Hizmet Movement could be seen as a part of the stabilization of democracy in Turkey. There is simply no concept of an Islamic state or Islamic revolution in the discourse inspired by Gülen, and the movement has avoided political engagement as much as possible (Saribay 1995). Yavuz (2004) goes further to state that for Gülen, it is anti-Islamic to talk about an Islamic state.

This approach has been welcomed by Turkish politicians of all kinds (Yavuz 2004). Gülen has met with a variety of political leaders and received the government's support regardless of the party in power.

NOTES

1. According to a survey conducted by Dr. Akbar Ahmed in 2007, Gülen was regarded as a role model by the majority of the respondents (Ahmed, 2007).

2. In Turkey, high school graduates take a nationwide test to get into the universities. Students are placed to universities according to their test scores from this nationwide test. Currently more than 1.5 million students take that test and a small number of them has chance to get a good education, therefore it is very common (almost all) for high school students to go to these private college preparatory centers *(dersane)* and study for the nationwide test.

3. All the magazines and news paper are best sellers in Turkey in their fields. For instance, Zaman Newspaper has a daily circulation close to a million.

4. Such as John Esposito &Hakan Yavuz (2003), Ihsan Yilmaz (2003), Heon Kim (2005), Zeki Saritoprak (2005), Thomas Michel (2005).

5. Sufi orders were banned in Turkey after the establishment of new secular state, but the teachings live within the culture.

6. Elisabeth Ozdagla (2005) defines the movement as a social network which is different that traditional Sufi lodges.

7. Gülen even does not accept being a leader of the movement or any group (Özkök, 1995).

8. Aras and Caha (2000) explains the Ottoman-Turkish understanding as follow:

> Islam in Turkish political history, during the reigns of both the Seljuks and the Ottomans, remained under the state's guidance and as a matter for the private sphere. The dominant belief was that a truly religious sultan would govern the state according to the principles of justice, equality, and piety. This approach of keeping religion apart from worldly affairs led to a collective memory that regarded Islam as a flexible and tolerant belief system. Thus, it was assumed that religious institutions should adopt flexible attitudes toward the changing situations of their times. In the Ottoman era, there was never a full-fledged theocratic system. While the principles of *Shari'a* (Islamic law) were applied in the private sphere, public life was regulated according to customary law formulated under the authority of the state (Berkes, 1998). This aspect of the Ottoman political system made religion's role less rigid. Moreover, the empire accepted it would be a multi-religious state, in which Christian and Jewish subjects would continue to be governed by their own laws.

9. Currently the number of the private schools in Turkey exceeded 150 (Agai 2005).

10. Students of these schools successfully represent Turkey in International Science Olympiads, as well as their schools in nationwide tests. A student from Yamanlar High School won the first international medal in the history of Turkish high schools.

11. Not only in Turkey, schools throughout the world, have been very successful in international science Olympiads.

12. Diyalog ve hosgoru in Turkish.

13. Yunus Emre (c.1238-c. 1320): A poet and Sufi who had a powerful influence on Turkish literature. He was well versed in Sufi philosophy especially that of Rumi, and like Rumi, became a leading representative of Sufism in Anatolia (but on a more popular level) (Gülen, 2004 p.46).

14. In both arguments Gülen uses Qur'an and the Hadith as his main resources.

Chapter 3

Defamation of Gülen in Turkish

In the defamatory articles and books published in Turkish, Gülen is portrayed as a puppet of American or Zionist power, used by westerners to destroy Turkey and exploit Muslim populations. Some of these articles even argue that Gülen works for the papacy and is not Muslim. Although a few early articles charge that Gülen is trying to establish an Islamic state in the secular Turkish Republic, by the end of 1990's, the majority of Turkish accusations tended in the opposite direction.

These Turkish defamations rely on several motifs: the image of the American puppet, the accusation that interfaith dialogue serves the Vatican, and the suggestion that Gülen's alleged Zionism will subvert Islam.

3.1.1. AMERICAN PUPPET: BIG MIDDLE EAST PROJECT

One accusation commonly made against Gülen is that he is being used by the American government. While some articles suggest that Gülen works directly for the CIA or another American paramilitary organization, others claim that America is using Gülen in order to promote a "softer" Islam not resist American exploitation of the Muslim world. According to this line of reasoning, Gülen's "moderate Islam" is really an American plot to subvert the economic and political strength of Muslim nations.

Dogu Perincek, the editor in chief of the magazine *Aydinlik,* is one of the leading figures to claim that Gülen is a CIA agent and working with "Super NATO" (Perincek 2007, Perincek 1996). According to this story, America has established paramilitary organizations in most of the NATO member countries, and these groups, known as "Super NATO" or "Gladio," are supposedly acting behind the scene to protect American interests. "Gladio" is allegedly responsible for the assassinations, murders, and coup d états that occur in these countries (Perincek 2007).

Authors who allege that Gülen is working for America typically make reference to "Buyuk Ortadogu Projesi," which translates as the "Big Middle East Project." They claim that America is trying to redesign the Middle East and change the borders between countries. The idea is that Fethullah Gülen and the Turkish Prime minister Recep Tayyip Erdogan are co-presidents of this secret American project, but Fethullah Gülen is its most effective leader. Ever since Turkey's entrance into NATO, this "Super NATO" conspiracy has been ruling the country. Even today's Ergenekon[1] case is explained as a "Super NATO" operation masterminded somehow by Gülen. (Yanardag 2007, Yanardag 2006, Veren 2007, Sezgin 2005) (Perincek 2007, Perincek 1996, E. Koc 2006, E. Koc 2006, Deniz 2007, Kizilkan 2008) (see Appendix for the full list of the references) For example:

> Super NATO told Tayyip Erdogan that it is going to make Diyarbakir the center of the second Israel, which is going to be established in Northern Iraq. Erdogan's co-presidency for the Big Middle East Project was a duty given to him by the Super NATO and by the deep state. The leader of this deep state is Fethullah and Tayyip; and the Fethullahist gangs who are positioned in the police system are the members of this deep state (Perincek 2007 p.3).

In addition to the accusations in newspaper and magazine articles, several books have been published in this vein. Himet Cetinkaya, Merdan Yanardag, and Ergun Poyraz are the most popular purveyors of this story. Hikmet Cetinkaya wrote "Fethullah Gülen's 40 year Adventure-1 and 2"(H. Cetinkaya 2004, H. Cetinkaya 2005); "Fethullah Gülen, USA and AKP" (H. Cetinkaya, Fethullah Gülen ABD ve AKP 2007); "Geese of Religion Baron" (H. Cetinkaya, Din Baron'un Kazlari 2006); "Fethullahist Gladio" (H. Cetinkaya, Fethullahçı Gladyo 2008); "American Harmonica Players" (H. Cetinkaya, Amerikan Mızıkacıları 2009); "Soros' Children" (H. Cetinkaya 2008).

Ergun Poyraz published: "Imam in America" (Poyraz, Amerika'daki mam 2009); "Those who do Wudu (ablution) with Blood" (Poyraz 2007); "Real Face of Fethullah" (Poyraz 2000); "From Said-i Nursi to Demirel and Ecevit: Fethullah's Real Face" (Poyraz 2000).

Merdan Yanardag also published several books in this regard: "How Turkey Besieged: Backstage of the Fethullah Gülen Movement" (Yanardag 2006); "AKP as an USA Project" (Yanardag 2007) (see Appendix for the full list of the books).

Some even claim that CIA agents are working in the Hizmet Movement schools as English teachers, especially in the Central Asian countries (Acik

Istihbarat 2010). Duyar (1998) claims that America has provided official diplomatic passports to more than 1000 Turkish teachers at Gülen schools.

3.1.2. MODERATE ISLAM: POPE'S SECRET CARDINAL

A more common motif in the Turkish defamatory articles and books is that Gülen has some sort of secret agreement with the Pope. His interfaith activities and moderate form of Islam are attempts to destroy Islam and Christianize all Muslims (Yilan 2006, Bala 2006).

Aziz Karaca and Emin Koc from the *Yeni Mesaj* newspaper are committed most vocally to this theme. They have prepared numerous newspaper articles suggesting that Gülen is employed by the Vatican and seeks to destroy Islam. Gülen's meeting with Pope John Paul II in 1998 is often put forward as official proof of this connection, and Poyraz (2000) goes on to claims that this meeting was arranged by the CIA. In the article "Curse to Those Who Opened This Way," Karaca (2006) writes:

> The children of the Muslim Turkish Nation, which has carried the flag of Islam for a thousand years, are moving towards trinity and polytheism [Christianity]...Polytheist, Crusade and Zionist union who could not defeat this nation [Muslim Turkish Nation] in battle is working to surrender this nation from inside and make them their tool by destroying their faith. ...Government's love of the EU, and dialogue team [Gülen Movement] who is part of Vatican council's mission have prepared everything for missioners and with their treason plans, they push our people to the missioners' arms and made our people an open market for them.

In his book *Vatican and Knights Templar*, Aytunc Altindal states that Pope John Paul II reactivated the Vatican's "dialogue project" in the 1990's. After discussing how Gülen's dialogue activities in Turkey seem to line up with the Vatican's projects, he writes:

> On February 21, 1998, Pope John Paul II appointed 20 new cardinals to the Vatican Senate...[In addition to these 20 cardinals] Pope John Paul II also used his right to appoint 'in pecture' two secret cardinals. This right has not been used by any pope for more than a hundred years.... Only seven people know the identities of these two cardinals... if they reveal their identities they will be killed in their countries... It is guessed that one of these 'in pecture' cardinals (who belong to other religions and hide their identities) is a religious leader in China... May the other one be a king/leader or a religious leader in the Muslim world? (Altindal 2004 p.115-7)

3.1.3. ZIONIST CONNECTIONS

In these accusations, Gülen is portrayed not as a puppet of the CIA or a secret cardinal, but as a Zionist partner working with MOSSAD and Israel. Some articles boldly claim that Gülen and leading members of the AKP government are actually "crypto-Jews" (people with Jewish decedents who are hiding their identities), while others merely suggest that he works secretly for Zionists groups (Poyraz 2000, Eraydin 2007, Biskin 2007, Sezgin 2007).

In 2007, Ergun Poyraz wrote *Moses' Children,* a series of books in which he "proves" that President Abdullah Gul, Prime Minister Tayyip Erdogan, AKP's leading figure Bulent Arinc, and Gülen are all Jewish. These books have titles like *Moses' AKP, Moses' Gul, Moses' Children Tayyip and Emine,* and so on[2] (Poyraz 2007, Poyraz 2007, Poyraz 2007, Poyraz 2007).

Riza Zelyut (2007) refers to the ADL (Anti Defamation League) as a Jewish organization that protects and promotes Gülen. He also claims that the ADL arranged for Gülen's meeting with the Pope John Paul II and for the publication and distribution of his books. In an article titled "Gülen, RTE (Recep Tayyip Erdogan) and their Cohort are ADL Servants," Emin Koc (2005) repeats the same arguments and claims that the ADL arranged for the distribution of Fethullah Gülen's *Love and Tolerance* around the world. Some go even further and claim that Bnai-Brith gives away all of Gülen's books for free (Acik Istihbarat n.d.).

Milli Cozum's Reseach Team has prepared a "Gülen File" and in which they underscore the similarities between the Gülen Movement and the Unification Church[3], claiming that both groups are organized by the Zionist CSIS (Center for Strategic and International Studies) (Milli Gorus Research Team 2004).

3.1.4. DESTROYING ISLAM: GÜLEN IS NOT A MUSLIM

A less common, but nonetheless present, motif in these Turkish defamations is that Gülen is not a sincere Muslim, but rather a hypocrite who seeks to radically alter Islam from inside (Poyraz 2000, E. Koc 2006). Some articles adopt the crypto-Jew approach, or the secret cardinal story, but all suggest that Gülen knows little about Islam and has intentions to corrupt large groups of Muslims. In his new book "Imam in America," Poyraz (2009) claims that Gülen's knowledge of Islam is limited and poor. According to Poyraz, Gülen does not even know basic things such as essentials of salah (prayer), and he does not have any knowledge of the Islamic mazhabs (Jurisprudence) and their imams. In his book titled *Fethullah Musluman mi?,* or *Is Fethullah*

Muslim?, Semih Tufan Gulaltay claims that Fethullah Gülen is actually Bahai, and marshalls a variety of "evidences" to support his accusation (Gulaltay n.d.). Senoglu and Bolat (2007) argue that Fethullah Gülen's fatwa has resulted in the removal of the Prophet Muhammed's name from the Shahada.[4]

In addition to aforementioned themes, some articles even claim that Gülen works with the Kurdish separatists group PKK and its leader Abdullah Ocalan (A. Akgul 2009, Ekmekci 2008, Gozubuyuk 2009).

NOTES

1. Ergenekon is the name given to an alleged clandestine, ultra-nationalist organization in Turkey with ties to members of the country's military and security forces. Many security and military personnel including retired generals have been arrested and it is an ongoing investigation. For more information see (Bozkurt 2010, Today's Zaman 2009).

2. Prime Minister Tayyip Erdogan's wife Emine Erdogan.

3. Known as also Moon Order.

4. The Shahada is the Muslimdeclaration of belief in the oneness of Allah and acceptance of Muhammad as God's prophet. It reads as *"There is no god but God, and Muhammad is the messenger of God."*

Chapter 4

Defamation of Gülen in English

With only a few exceptions, defamatory articles in English portray Gülen as an Islamic danger to Western world. He is accused of trying to establish an Islamic caliphate through a strategy of religiously-sanctioned dissimulation (taqiyya). According to these articles, Gülen is both anti-Western and anti-Semitic, and his promotion of tolerance, understanding, and interfaith dialogue is simply meant to disguise his true intentions of establishing a secret caliphate.

As was the case in the Turkish articles, several motifs are systematically repeated throughout the English defamations. These are characterized by references to a "Trojan Horse," fears that moderate Islam and interfaith dialogue disguise more nefarious intentions, comparisons to Khomeini. Gülen is variously accused of trying to overthrow the secular Turksih government and found an Islamic state, resurrect the New Ottoman Empire, establish a universal caliphate, and infiltrate the United States in order to train Islamist militia. Most of the defamatory English articles present some combination of these motifs, often citing as evidence other defamatory texts in a self-referential loop.

In the sections that follow, the leading authors responsible for these accusations are categorized by motif. For a complete list of English articles, see the Appendix.

4.1. ISLAM'S TROJAN HORSE:
MODERATE ISLAM AS TAQIYYA

One of the earliest defamatory articles written in English came from Paul Stenhouse at Quadrant. After the establishment of a Fethullah Gülen Chair of

Islamic Studies and Interfaith Dialogue at the Australian Catholic University in Melbourne's Centre of Inter-Religious Dialogue, Stenhouse (2007) raised questions about Gülen, stating that the Gülen Movement is a "group that is ex professo dedicated to promoting an Islamist ideology." As implied by his title, "Islam's Trojan Horse? Turkish Nationalism and the Nakshibendi Sufi Order," Stenhouse asserts that despite its promotion of tolerance and interfaith dialogue, the Gülen Movement really harbors a hidden Islamist agenda.[1]

Articles which insist on some sort of hidden agenda often refer to a fabricated video record of Gülen.[2] The typical accusation is that Gülen justifies taqiyya (religiously-sanctioned dissimulation), in order that his followers can secretly infiltrate Western society (Fitzgerald 2008, Rubin 2008, Sharon-Krespin 2009, Stenhouse 2007, Mizell 2008). And in such accounts, the Hizmet Movement is often labeled a "secret cult" rather than a social movement.

4.2. AMERICA'S KHOMEINI: SAME EVIL DIFFERENT BEARD

Michael Rubin is another leading author of the inciting articles. In "Turkey's Turning Point" from the National Review Online, Rubin (2008) claims that Gülen will eventually establish an Islamic state in Turkey, just like Khomeini in Iran:

> As Khomeini consciously drew parallels between himself and Twelver Shiism's Hidden Imam, Gülen will remain quiet as his supporters paint his return as evidence that the caliphate formally dissolved by Atatürk in 1924 has been restored (Rubin 2008).

In a recent article, Rubin (2010) repeats his claims and defines Gülen as "a cult leader, and the closest thing Turkey has to Khomeini-in-exile." But this time, he takes his accusations a step further, asserting that Gülen is "an Islamist cult leader maintaining a compound staffed and secured by machine-gun-wielding thugs in the mountains of Pennsylvania."

Fitzgerald (2008) also compares Gülen to Ayatollah Khomeini in a similar way, cautioning the United States against "moderate Islamists." According to Fitzgerald, Gülen is more dangerous than Khomeini because he is "cunning, clever, and very, very sinister." He claims that Turkey has already succumbed to Fethullah Gülen's control, but he chooses to stay in the United States as a part of his ambitious strategy:

Now that Turkey is going just as Fethullah Gülen wished, you may ask why he doesn't fly home to a hero's welcome. And the answer is that he now has other, and bigger, fish to fry. He has the entire Western world to help conquer from within (Fitzgerald 2008).

4.3. OVERTHROWING TURKISH SECULAR GOVERNMENT AND ESTABLISHING AN ISLAMIC STATE

This motif of a looming Islamic state recurs in almost all of the defamatory English articles. Gülen is accused first trying to overthrow the existing secular state in Turkey, after which he will found an Islamic state that will encompass the entire world.

Rachel Sharon-Krespin's (Sharon-Krespin 2009) article titled "Fethullah Gülen's Grand Ambition: Turkey's Islamist Danger" is to blame for much of this suspicion. Sharon-Krespin's article, written as if it were an academic paper, was published by Middle East Quarterly. While the article purports to analyze objective data gathered on Fethullah Gülen and the Hizmet Movement, Sharon-Krespin consciously manipulates evidence to systematically defame Gülen. But given its apparent prestige, the article has been referenced numerous times by subsequent libels, inspiring many of the groundless fears that permeate such documents. Sharon-Krespin (2009) claims:

Today, despite the rhetoric of European Union accession, Prime Minister Recep Tayyip Erdoğan has turned Turkey away from Europe and toward Russia and Iran and reoriented Turkish policy in the Middle East away from sympathy toward Israel and much more toward friendship with Hamas, Hezbollah, and Syria. Anti-American, anti-Christian, and anti-Semitic sentiments have increased. Behind Turkey's transformation has been not only the impressive AKP (Adelet ve Kalkinma Partisi- Justice and Development Party) political machine but also a shadowy Islamist sect led by the mysterious *hocaefendi* (master lord) Fethullah Gülen; the sect often bills itself as a proponent of tolerance and dialogue but works toward purposes quite the opposite. Today, Gülen and his backers (*Fethullahcılar*, Fethullahists) not only seek to influence government but also to become the government.

Gurdogan (2010) echoes these suspicions, depicting the Gülen Movement as a "danger spreading from Turkey to the world." He makes a point of noting that Gülen Movement is really a "secret cult" that is slowly taking over the Turkish government in partnership with the current governing party AKP. He claims:

...this cult [Gülen Movement] ensures that those members who join them end up pledging their allegiance while they are at young ages; paving the way for them to get a proper education and prepare them so they can get any position at government agencies. With this method, they avoid a direct conflict and argument between the state and themselves, and simultaneously place cult members into the various government agencies, also known as Trojan horses, and have them act completely in the interest of the cult in order to help "capture" the agencies they are working inside of (Gurdogan 2010).

4.4. RESURRECTION OF NEW OTTOMAN EMPIRE, AND UNIVERSAL CALIPHATE

The idea that Gülen seeks a resurrection of the Ottoman Empire or the establishment of a new Ottoman Empire and universal caliphate appears in a number of the defamatory English articles. However, Aland Mizell and Paul Williams[3] are clearly the lead purveyors of such a notion.

Mizell has written several articles addressing Gülen and the Gülen Movement, all of them defamatory. In one of his early articles, "The Rise of a New Ottoman Empire: The Trap of the Interfaith Dialogue," he writes:

Gülen believes that since the Ottoman Empire ruled the world for many centuries with peace, he wants to bring it back again. By creating big lobbies, Gülen moves toward his ultimate goal of dictating American and Western social, political, and economic policies. He has recruited thousands of teachers and millions of students while raising billions of dollars in economic support" (Mizell 2008).

Two years later, Mizell (2010) repeats his claims:

today, the Ottoman Empire is back. Now the Ottoman proponents--like Fethullah Gülen and his followers—want to reverse everything Ataturk did. A variety of Islamic groups have tried various platforms to impose their power over people, but today the twenty-first century tactic of raising up leaders with a radical agenda of reinstating the Turkish Ottoman's core of Islam under the guise of an educational system is regressing the country toward the pre-republic days.

Among the many incendiary claims of Paul Williams (2010) his one that Gülen is using "his" schools to raise a new generation of Islamists who will restore the Ottoman Empire:

The most dangerous Islamist in the world is neither Afghani nor Arab. He comes from neither Sudan nor Somalia. And he resides in neither the mountains

of Pakistan nor the deserts of the Palestinian territories. This individual has top-
pled the secular government of Turkey and established madrassahs throughout
the world. His schools indoctrinate children in the tenets of radical Islam and
prepare adolescents for the Islamization of the world...Dozens of his universities, including the Faith University in Istanbul, train young men to become law-
yers, accountants, and political leaders so that they can take an active part in the
restoration of the Ottoman Empire and the Islamization of the Western World.

In the same article, Williams (2010) claims that Gülen "has amassed a
fortune—over $30 billion—for the creation of a universal caliphate."

David Goldman (2010) joins Mizell and Williams with his own claims that
Gülen's vision of moderate Islam is a "magical, mystic's vision of Ottoman
restoration and a pan-Turkic caliphate." He also asserts that Gülen "is a sha-
man, a relic of pre-history preserved in the cultural amber of eastern Anatolia...who inhabits the magical world of *jinns* and sorcery and sees science as
a powerful form of magic of which Turks should avail themselves to enhance
their power" (Goldman 2010).

4.5. INFILTRATION INTO THE UNITED STATES

A wide range of articles, internet comments, blogs, and websites have been
dedicated to the suspicion that Fethullah Gülen is infiltrating the United
States through charter schools, and that he uses publicly financed education
to pursue his agenda of Turkish religio-political indoctrination (Schwartz
2010, Rodgers 2010).

One of the first articles of this type was produced by Guy Rodgers for
the Act for America website in early 2010. Rodgers claims that Fethullah
Gülen, a dangerous Islamist leader, has been using charter schools to secretly
proselytize in the United States. He even claims that the Department of
Homeland Security had tried to deport him but could not succeed. According
to Rodgers, the Fethullah Gülen Community runs over 90 public schools in at
least 20 states, and these schools, though disguised as science academies and
excelling academically, are in fact "doing an excellent job of heeding Gülen's
exhortation and masking their true intent" (Rodgers 2010). He continues:

> In building a sophisticated and well-funded worldwide network, including a
> substantial presence here in the U.S., Fethullah Gülen is following in the foot-
> steps and exhortations of Mohammed, who counseled patience and deception
> as a means of overcoming the infidel when the power of the infidel was greater
> than the power of the *umma*, the Muslim community. In a very real sense this
> is as or more sinister than the frontal assault strategy of Islamist organizations
> such as al Qaeda and Hamas, because, like the proverbial "frog in the kettle,"

we are incrementally "boiled alive" without realizing it.The FGC charter schools in America may outwardly appear innocuous, but they are serving a greater and long-range objective of Fethullah Gülen.

4.6. TRAINING ISLAMIST MILITIA IN THE UNITED STATES

One accusation made on some anti-Gülen blogs and websites is that Gülen is currently training an Islamist militia in the United States. Paul Williams and Roberto Santiago have repeatedly suggested that Gülen's compound in Pennsylvania is being used for such a purpose:

> Christian militias have been raided in Michigan and Ohio, their members rounded up and tossed in prison and their caches of weapons confiscated. But a well-armed Muslim militia—comprised not of American citizens but foreign militants—operates under the noses of federal and state law enforcement officials. If you don't it, pay a visit to Saylorsburg, Pennsylvania, in the heart of the Pocono Mountains (Williams 2010).

Williams also states that Fethullah Gülen "allegedly operates compounds to train jihadis in the tactics of guerilla warfare" (Williams 2010). In one of his online posts, he claims:

> …powerful Turkish pasha Fethullah Gülen has established a 45 acre mountain fortress. The fortress remains protected by 100 Turkish guards and a sentry post. Local residents have complained of automatic gunfire coming from the complex and of a low flying helicopter that surveys the area for would-be intruders (Williams 2010). [4]

NOTES

1. The term "Trojan Horse" has been used by almost all of the groups that are strategically trying to defame Gülen. It appears both in English and Turkish versions of the defamation articles. While Gülen is accused being Islam's Trojan Horse in the Western World/Christianity, in Turkish versions, he is accused of being West's/Pope's Trojan Horse in the Muslim World.

2. See Abdullah Ademoglu's (2010) "Defamation of Gülen as a Smoke Screen" article for more information on these fabricated records.

3. Paul Williams is an interesting figure in this defamation campaign, as he appears in a number of contexts. For more information see section Paul Williams: A Defamation Machine.

4. After the Williams artice, Pocono Record Writer, Dan Berrett visited the retreat center where Gülen lives. Berrett spoke to security officers and neighbors living in the neighborhood, and states: "None of the neighbors with whom the Pocono Record spoke said they had ever heard or seen what Williams described…'You couldn't meet a nicer bunch of people,' said Howard Beers Jr., a Ross Township supervisor who lives next door and enters the property six or seven days a week, often unannounced and not through the front gate, to do construction work. 'If anyone would walk in on something, it would be me,' Beers said. 'As long as I have ever been there, I have never, ever, seen a gun or heard a shot. All this stuff is totally, totally unfounded.' Efforts to reach Williams through the Web site and his blog were unsuccessful" (Berrett 2010).

Chapter 5

Data Analysis

5.1. DATA AND CODING:

In order to demonstrate the strategic nature of these defamations, I will define the two different sets of accusations as *Gülen1* and *Gülen2* and code the articles accordingly. *Gülen1* refers to the claims that Gülen is an American/Zionist/ Vatican agent (or more generally, anti-Islam), while *Gülen2* includes any accusations that make mention of Gülen as Islamist/Khomeini/New Ottoman/ Caliphate (anti-Western). The dataset includes 435 cases compiled from both English and Turkish sources that depict Gülen's activities in one of these two ways.

Data selection was also guided by Hankin's (2008) definition of defmation as "the communication of a statement that makes a claim, expressly stated or implied to be factual, that may give an individual, business, group, or nation a negative image." It is required that the claim be false and that the publication be directed toward someone other than the person defamed. Hankin lists five essential elements to defamation: "(1) the accusation is false; and (2) it impeaches the subject's character; and (3) it is published to a third person; and (4) it damages the reputation of the subject; and (5) that the accusation is done intentionally or with fault such as wanton disregard of facts."

In other words, articles that critize Gülen appropriately are not included in the dataset. For instance, Karaca's (2005) article titled "Diyalog meyveleri zehirliyor" (translated: "Fruits of Dialogue are Poisoning Us") is critical of Gülen, and especially of the dialogue activities organized by the the Hizmet Movement. However, Karaca states his own opinions that "dialogue activities are harming Muslim Turkish youth," and makes no false accusations against

Gülen or any members of the Hizmet movement. Therefore, this article is not included in the dataset. On the other hand, in his article titled "Diyaloga karşıyız, çünkü…" (translated: "We are against Dialogue, because…") Karaca (2005) not only criticizes Gülen's advocacy of dialogue, but he goes on to imply that Gülen is a part of a larger project developed by the Vatican to Christianize Muslims. Therefore, this article is included in the dataset.

If an article happens to include both defamatory depictions, it is included in the dataset twice and coded once for each accusation. For instance, in an article titled "Gülen Movement Paves Way For New Islamic World Order Billions Pour Into Gülen's Coffers From Drug Trade," Paul Williams describes Gülen as:

> …a Turk, who is intent upon the establishment of a universal caliphate, and a militant Islamist, who seeks to indoctrinate youth in the political teachings of the Qu'ran.

This description clearly qualifies the article to be coded as Gülen2. However, in the same article Paul Williams also claims that:

> The CIA has allowed the flow of heroin from Afghanistan into Europe and the United States in order to fund the Gülen movement.

This accusation of conspiracy between the United States and the Hizmet Movement is characteristic of other anti-Islam defamations, and so the article is also coded as Gülen1.

Especially among the English articles, there are high numbers of "reposts," in which the same article appears verbatim on different weblogs. For the sake of data coding, if the same article is posted without revision on several different weblogs, only the original article is included in the dataset. However, if the article is re-posted with additional comments, each version is included in the dataset and coded accordingly.

5.2. DATA ANALYSIS AND THE RESULTS

The statistics below reveal that in 98% of Turkish articles making defamatory claims, Gülen is depicted as American/Zionist/Vatican agent (Gülen1). In only 2% of the defamatory Turkish articles is Gülen considered Islamist/Khomeini/New Ottoman/Caliphate (Gülen2). But in the English defamations, the situation is reversed. While Gülen is portrayed as anti-Islam (Gülen1) in 11% of the defamatory English articles, he is presented as anti-Western (Gülen2) in 89% of them.

Table 5.1. Descriptive Statistics of the Data

	#*Gülen1*	#*Gülen2*	%*Gülen1*	%*Gülen2*
Turkish	340	7	%98	%2
English	10	78	%11	%89
TOTAL	350	85	%80	%20

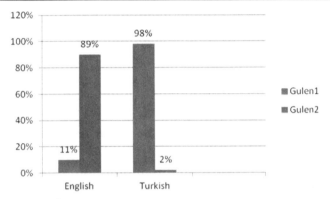

Figure 5.1. % Graph of Gülen1 and Gülen2 According to Languages

Taken together, Gülen is depicted as Gülen1 in 80% of all Turkish and English defamations, and as Gülen2 in 20% of the articles. This is simply because there are many more articles defaming Gülen in Turkish than English. If we consider the timeline presented in the graphics below, it is clear that this imbalance is due to the fact that the Turkish defamations came into circulation earlier than their English inverses. However, there has been a huge jump in the number of English defamations in recent years, and if this increase continues, it will not take long for incendiary articles to be equally common in both languages.

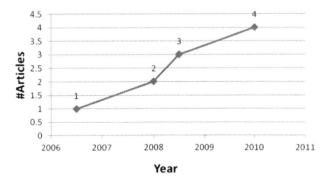

Figure 5.2. Gülen1 in English

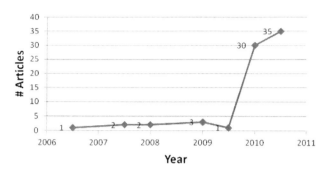

Figure 5.3. Gülen2 in English

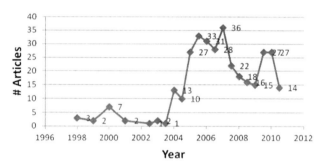

Figure 5.4. Gülen1 in Turkish

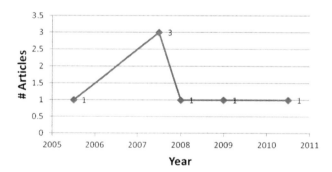

Figure 5.5. Gülen2 in Turkish

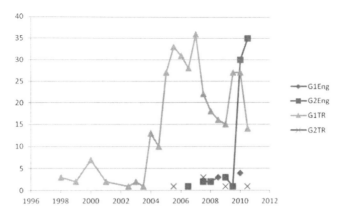

Figure 5.6. Both Gülen1 and Gülen2 in both Turkish and English

Timelines of data also show that Turkish defamers increased their attacks between 2006 and 2008; on the other hand, English version articles skyrocketed after the second half of 2009 and continue to increase. A recent report published by the Center for American Progess points out that there is a linked group of people in the United States that spends millions of dollars to create a false image for Muslims. Gülen also became one of their targets after the second half of 2009. Most of the authors mentioned in English defamatory section were listed in this report. This shows why there has been a huge increase in defamatory articles in English after 2009.

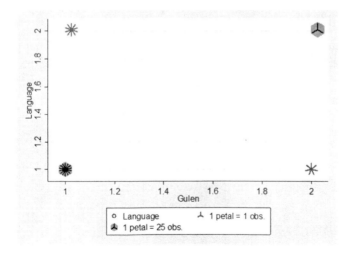

Figure 5.7. Sunflower Graph of Language and Gülen

Dark brown points show the concentrations of the observations. The above graph shows a concentration of articles in Turkish at Gülen1, and a concentration of articles in English at Gülen2. This is another way of saying that Gülen is mostly portrayed in Turkish as being anti-Islamic and in English as being anti-Western.

Correlation between the language and the picture of Gülen
(obs=435) (t=38.093) (p<0.0001)

	Language	Gülen
Language	1.0000	
Gülen	0.8776	1.0000

Gülen1 is coded as 1, Gülen2 is coded as 2; Turkish is coded as 1, English is coded as 2

A correlation test for the data demonstrates a correlation of .8776, which is a very strong positive correlation. There is a very high correlation between the depiction of Gülen and the Hizmet movement given in an article and the language that is the article is written in. In other words, most likely when the language is Turkish, Gülen is defamed as Gülen1, and when the language is English, as Gülen2. One can predict how Gülen is defamed with a 87% accuracy only by looking at the language of the article, regardless of the authors.

These results suggest that Gülen is defamed strategically, not randomly. The authors of such incendiary articles shape their depiction of Gülen according to the primary fears and suspicions of their particular audiences. The accusation that Gülen is involved in some American/Zionist/Vatican conspiracy plays off of the fears of Turkish readers, and therefore will produce a greater negative impression. Likewise, his defamation as a secret Islamist is likely to generate a greater negative impression among English readers. Therefore, authors who wish to denigrate the work of Gülen and the Hizmet movement resort to these contradictory defamations and model their accusations on the primary fears of their audience rather than any gathered evidence.

Chapter 6

Who are they?
Analysis of These Groups

6.1. TURKISH

Various groups in Turkey are opposed to Gülen and the Hizmet Movement, and the reasons for their opposition have been analyzed by Yavuz (2003; 2004), Cetin (2005), Ozdalga (2005), Saritoprak and Griffith (2005), Aslandogan (2006), Tedik (2007) among others. According to most of the literature on this subject, the antagonism towards Gülen originates from two groups: the secular elites and the radical Islamists. Each opposes the Hizmet Movement for different reasons, and from vastly different ideological perspectives. Radical Islamists in Turkey argue that the Gülen and the Hizmet Movement are humiliating Islam by engaging in dialogue with Christians and allowing Christians to proselytize Muslims. Gülen's meeting with Pope John Paul II in 1998 was criticized heavily by these minor radical Islamist groups for this reason (Saritoprak and Griffith 2005).

Turkish Islamist groups depict Gülen as a part of a western plot to infiltrate Turkey in particular and Islam in general. There have even been suggestions that the CIA may be a financial partner in various Hizmet Movement projects (Kalyoncu, 2008). Mehmet Sevket Eygi, the chief writer of the a right wing-Islamist daily newspaper *Milli Gazete*, has indirectly accused Gülen of being a secret agent of the Papacy (2000a, 2000b). And a similarly radical Islamist news paper *Yeni Mesaj* (New Message) ran articles stating that Muslims who advocate inter-religious dialogue with Christians and Europeans (referring the Hizmet Movement) were either naïve, ignorant, or treasonous (New Message, 2000a, 2000b, 2000c, 2000d).

But the strongest opposition to the Gülen Movement comes from Turkey's elite secularists: the 'hard-line secularists' in Saritoprak and Griffith (2005),

'Kemalist elites' in Yavuz (2004) and Tedik (2007), 'established ones' in Oz-dalga (2005), 'statist-elitist-leftist-militant' secularist groups in Cetin (2005). According to Tedik (2007), these are the people who generally hold high posts in the Turkish state, not so much as political officials, but as bureau-cratic figures (e.g. members of the military, high judicial organs etc.). Hakan Yavuz (2004) explains the reasons for their antagonism in an interview with *Religioscope*:

> Gülen represents a major threat for these people, because they want to see a backward, radical Islam, in order to justify repression—whereas with Gülen, you do not get that. This angers them even more! Also, Gülen tries to educate the periphery by teaching them foreign languages and providing scholarships for study in foreign countries. This angers the establishment as well, because they want to control the country and not to share the resources with the rest of the population. There is also a conflict over resources. Gülen was on the side of the poor, while the establishment did not want to see his movement opening up educational opportunities for the marginal sectors of Turkish society. This frustrated militant secularists in Turkey.

Elizabeth Ozdalga (2005) emphasizes the role played by a "conflict over resources." She describes the secularist elites as the "settled ones" who, de-spite their minority numbers, control the majority of the country's resources. Within this group, the Gülen Movement represents a change in the balance of power in favour of "those coming from outside," and the fear of such change motivates their opposition to the work of the Hizmet Movement.

Cetin (2005) identifies the same group of bureaucratic eliets as "statist-elitist-leftist-militant secularist." Cetin (2005) stresses that this ruling class directs its "aggressiveness at the Hizmet Movement in order to at least par-tially repair [a] sense of loss and to preserve the positiveness of their action in the eyes of the general public." According to Cetin (2005), their opposition towards Gülen is motivated by a fear of losing power.

Although these groups, both radical Islamists and ultra secularists elites come from opposite sides of the ideological spectrum, they agree that Gülen is a threat and produce texts that are almost identical in their defamatory claims. While the ultra-secular group tends to accuse Gülen of conspiracy with the American government, the radical Islamist groups emphasize Gül-en's alleged connection with the Vatican. But their defamatory strategies and motifs exhibit the remarkable consistency elaborated above.

The ultra-secularist, ultra-nationalist (ulusalci) group has strong ties with the Ergenekon Terrorist Organization, and some of its libelous authors have been arrested because of these connections. Ironically, these groups present themselves in opposite political and ideological positions, however, there are also evidences that these groups are connected with each other, and are coordinated by the Ergenekon Terrorist Organization (For more information on Ergenekon's Islamist arm see (Aytac and Uslu 2008, Aytac and Uslu 2008). On July 23, 2008, 28 people in 5 different cities from the *Milli Cozum* magazine (one of the radical Islamist outlets leading Gülen's defamation) were taken into custody due to connection with the Ergenekon Terrorist Organization (Internet Haber 2008).

Ergenekon is the name given to an alleged clandestine, ultra-secularist, ultra-nationalist organization in Turkey with ties to members of the country's military and security forces. Many security and military personnel, including some generals, have been arrested recently in the ongoing investigation. The members of the organization define themselves as defenders of secularism and national sovereignty, who have a legitimate authority over democratically elected governments for the protection of national interests of Turkey. They also claim that it is their right to usurp the power of the government (usually through a coup) whenever they see the democratically elected leaders not acting according to the "national interests," which they of course reserve the right to define.

Members of Ergenokon have been accused of instigating unrest by assassinating intellectuals, politicians, judges, military staff, and religious leaders, with the ultimate goal of toppling the incumbent government (Burke 2008, Rainsford 2008, Düzel 2008). Prosecutors claim links between Ergenekon and the killing of a Turkish Council of State judge in 2006, the bombing of a secularist newspaper, the killings of several high ranking military personnel, the murder of a prominent Turkish-Armenian journalist (Hrant Dink), the murder of Italian priest Father Andrea Santora, and brutal murder of three Christian missionaries in 2007 in Malatya, and thousands of other unsolved murder cases.

Documents seized in the investigation show that the group planned a bomb attack in Istanbul's Taksim Square to trigger chaos that would be used as a pretext for military intervention. It is also alleged that those detained were involved in provocation and agitation during the Gazi incidents of 1995, in which dozens of people died in clashes with the police while demonstrating after an attack at an Alevi coffeehouse (Balci and Karabat 2009).

It is assumed that Ergenekon's intention is to discredit the incumbent Justice and Development Party and derail Turkey's accession to the EU. Ergenekon's agenda has variously been described as Eurasianist and isolationist, and the group is strongly opposed to the possibility of Turkey's membership in the EU and further integration with the West (Uslu 2008, Balci 2008). Journalist Nazli Ilicak (2009) defines the goals of Ergenekon as following:

[Ergenekon's] goal is to sustain 'stability' by overthrowing the unwanted AKP [Justice and Development Party], to govern the state with a Ba'athist system, and to align Turkey with Russia by breaking off ties with the US and the EU. In their protests, the message was: "Neither EU nor US, but independent Turkey!

In the ongoing investigation, there is strong evidence emerging that the members of Ergenekon have orchestrated at least four military coups in the last decade in order to achieve their goals.

Both of these anti-Gülen groups deny the Ergenekon case and try to show that this is an American operation. They both are pro-military; they both oppose the US and the EU; they both are ultranationalist, anti-Semitic, anti-Christian, anti-minorities.[1] According to them, the United States is behind most of the killings and chaos in Turkey. The US is controlling all these activities through its Super NATO structures within Turkey (Ulusal TV 2009). For them, in order to clean 'national powers' within the Turkish Army, United States has started and controlling the Ergenekon case.

6.1.1. ULTRA-SECULARIST, ULTRA-NATIONALIST (ULUSALCI) GROUP

Although there are many authors, websites, and magazines dedicated to the defamation of Gülen, a few stand out as prominent voices within the ultra-secular, ultra-nationalist (ulusalci) group in Turkey: Hikmet Cetinkaya, Ergun Poyraz, and Dogu Perincek (the Aydinlik Group).

Hikmet Cetinkaya: A Career Dedicated to Gülen's Defamation

Hikmet Cetinkaya has been writing about Gülen more than three decades, and Webb (2003) identifies him as one of Fethullah Gülen's most relentless enemies. Although earlier in his career he accused Gülen of trying to establish an Islamic state and bring shari'a to Turkey, in last decade he has been portraying Gülen as an American agent.[2]

Hikmet Cetinkaya is a staunch ultra-secularist. Since his student life, he has been strongly pro-military and supportive of the coup d'états in Turkey. Since 1966, Cetinkaya has been writing at the *Cumhuriyet* newspaper, one of the oldest in Turkey, which is known for its ultra-secularist and elitist approach. Although it was founded in 1924, *Cumhuriyet* is currently one of the least circulated newspapers in Turkey, with a daily circulation of fifty thousand, and has become the marginal news outlet for a small group of ultra–secularists. *Cumhuriyet's* late editor in chief Ilhan Selcuk and Ankara Bureau Chief Mustafa Balbay were detained in 2008 as suspected members of the Ergenekon Terrorist Organization. Ilhan Selcuk was accused of being he one of the masterminds behind the latest coup attempts, but he was released due to old age and health problems and placed on trial without an arrest. Ilhan Selcuk died on June 21, 2010 at the age of 85 due to multiple organ failures.

At *Cumhuriyet,* Hikmet Cetinkaya has written hundreds of newspaper articles and several books about Gülen and the Hizmet Movement. Ten of his books explicitly promote a defamatory picture of Gülen, in which Cetinkaya's main argument is that Gülen is representative of an American-led "moderate Islamic" project. According to Cetinkaya, Gülen established a relationship with America in the 1980's in exchange for permission to open schools in Central Asia. Cetinkaya (2009) also claims that the Hizmet Movement schools in Northern Iraq were opened with the help of CIA, and that the school materials were carried into the Northern Iraq by the Red Cross (H. Cetinkaya 2009). In his analysis of Cetinkaya's articles, Turker (2009) states:

> In one of his news pieces, Cetinkaya quotes İlhan Selçuk, editor-in-chief of *Cumhuriyet*: "Fethullah Gülen, who is living in America, is the vein of Christian imperialism in the Muslim world; while he is playing an oppressed religious role, in reality, he is playing for politics [and] business because he leans his back on neocon evangelists and is controlled by them, money, finance...

In the same article, Çetinkaya claims that Gülen is supported by the CIA. To make his point, he gives the example of a school in Arbil in northern Iraq. According to Çetinkaya, 25 of the 40 teachers working at that school had American passports in 1994.

The titles of some of Cetinkaya's other books on Gülen make his position clear: Fethullah Gülen's 40 Year Adventure; Fethullahist Gladio; American Harmonica Players; Children of Soros; Bigot and Conjuror.

Ergun Poyraz: Turkish Defamation Machine

In 2000, Ergun Poyraz became one of the first authors to publish a book defaming Gülen, titled "Fethullah's Real Face." Like Cetinkaya, he also asserts that Fethullah Gülen works for the United States, but primarily alleges Zionist connections.

Poyraz is known for his anti-semitic series of "Moses' X" books, which are uniformly titled: Moses' Children, Moses' AKP (Justice and Development Party), Moses' Gul (Turkish President Abdullah Gul), Moses' Children Tayyip and Emine (Turkish Prime Minster Recep Tayyip Erdogan and his wife Emine Erdogan), and so on.

In this series, Poyraz "proves" that the leaders of the Justice and Development Party, as well as Gülen and several others, are crypto-Jews working for Israel and the United States (Poyraz 2007, Poyraz 2007, Poyraz 2007). Such "secret Jews" allegedly use Turkish and Muslim identities to disguise their true intentions. It is interesting that, while Turkish authors accuse Gülen of working for Israel and America, English authors accuse him of being anti-Semitic and anti-American (compare Poyraz to Sharon-Krespin[3]).

Much like Paul Williams, Ergun Poyraz is a veritable defamation factory. He has published dozens of books accusing Fethullah Gülen and various leaders of Justice and Development Party of conspiracy with Israel and the US. In 2007 alone, he published six books to this effect.

Not surprisingly, Ergun Poyraz was arrested on July 27, 2007 for his connections with the Ergenekon Terrorist Organization. At a later investigation of the Worker's Party's headquarters, a CD documenting details of Poyraz's connections with JITEM.[4] According to these documents, Ergun Poyraz received a regular salary from JITEM, which links him with the Ergenekon organization. Official documents were found which contained the amount of monthly payments as well as the names and signatures of army officers who approved them. When General Sener Eruygur (who is detained in the Ergenekon case) was the commander of the General Command of Gendarmerie, thousands of copies of Poyraz's books were bought by the Gendarmerie and distributed among military units (Sahin 2010).

Dogu Perincek (Aydinlik Group)

Dogu Perincek is the head of the Worker's Party, a communist, nationalist, and pro-Russian party with very little support in Turkey, and *Aydinlik* (enlightenment) is its weekly magazine. This group has produced dozens of articles in which, as is the case with other defamations, Gülen is portrayed as a CIA and MOSSAD agent.

Aydinlik has presented one of the most marginal and bizarre claims about Gülen. According to the articles in *Aydinlik* magazine, the CIA has admitted its affiliation with Gülen and openly protects him (2002). These authors suppose that when Turkey and Russia began operations against the CIA and MOSSAD within the region, the CIA and MOSSAD countered with a number of assassinations, including the murder of Necip Hablemitoglu.[5] *Aydinlik* magazine claims that Gülen was working with MOSSAD and the CIA at this time. In another issue of *Aydinlik*, the ex-prosecutor Vural Savas writes:

> I believe that the murders of Kemalist intellectuals such as Muammer Aksoy, Ugur Mumcu, Ahmet Taner Kislali, and Necip Hablemitoglu are the works of imperialist states and their intelligence organizations (CIA/MOSSAD), and the Fethullahist network within the Turkish police is the biggest barrier to the investigation of these murders (Savas 2007).

In other words, Savas (2007) asserts that CIA and MOSSAD killed these Kemalist intellectuals, and Fethullah Gülen's network has worked within the police to prepare the scene for these killings.

Although Dogu Perincek and the *Aydinlik* group are themselves very anti-Islam, when it comes to Fethullah Gülen, they claim to be protecting Islam from "Fethullah Gülen's attacks." They criticize Fethullah Gülen's dialogue activities, claiming that he is controlled by the Vatican. These dialogue activities are alleged to "Christ-centered" with no place for Muhammad:

> The essence of dialogue is Jesus Christ centered Christianity. Those who want to establish dialogue with Christians have to revolve around Jesus and not approach Muhammed. Thus, the Beyond-Atlantic Group[6] (Hizmet Movement) and groups who have joined them put Muhammed's name in parenthesis (they ignore the name), because there cannot be a Jesus Christ centered dialogue where Muhammed exists.
>
> Fethullah Gülen is working with Israel's Chief Rabbi Bahsi Doron. Gülen, as an "advocate of dialogue," seems to be more of an advocate of imperialism. Like Saint Paul of Christianity, he has transformed the 'be everything to everyone' into an economic, political, and religious philosophy (Filiz 2007).

According to *Aydinlik* magazine, Gülen gave a fatwa removing Muhammed's name from the Islamic Shahada in order to be able to have a Jesus centered dialogue (Senoglu and Bolat 2007).

On 21 March 2008, Dogu Perincek was detained for his membership in Ergenekon alongside several other authors from *Aydinlik* magazine and the leadership of Worker's Party. Perincek was arrested and accused of being one of the high ranking leaders of the Ergenekon Terrorist Organization.

6.1.2. Radical Islamist Group

While the aforementioned authors are the leading figures of the ultra-nationalist, ultra-secularist group opposing Gülen, there are also several authors attacking Gülen from the perspective of radical Islam. The most prominent among them are Aziz Karaca of the *Yeni Mesaj* (New Message) newspaper and Ahmet Akgul from the *Milli Cozum* (National Solution) magazine.

Aziz Karaca and the Yeni Mesaj *Group:*

Aziz Karaca and the *Yeni Mesaj* group are especially antagonistic towards Gülen's interfaith dialogue activities. According to them, the activity of interfaith dialogue throughout the world is a Vatican project developed in order to Christianize members of other faiths, especially Muslims. They suspect that the Vatican uses interfaith dialogue to disguise its missionary activities (Karaca 2005, Karaca 2006, E. Koc 2005). Therefore, anybody who is involved with interfaith dialogue must either be assisting the spread of Christianity or worse, working directly for the Vatican.

While they consider the majority of the members of the Hizmet Movement to be merely deceived, the *Yeni Mesaj* group considers Gülen to be a partner or subcontractor in the Vatican's work. They believe that Christian missionaries are secretly active all over Turkey, opening dozens of churches, distributing thousands of free bibles, and converting hundreds of young people to Christianity. Soon, they fear, Turkey will be invaded from inside (Karaca 2005). And Gülen is Vactican's "Trojan horse" who allows for and encourages such subversion:

> Those who knows the history of Vatican, knows very well that Vatican would not water any fruit tree which would not have Vatican's color, smell, and taste [in other words, Vatican does not get involved with any business if it is not its own business]. If Vatican's late Pope greeted and honored this dialogue grounds man [Gülen] with special compliments, that's why all the dialogue fruits grown by this dialogue grounds man point to Vatican (Karaca 2005).

Of course, the Vatican is not the only outside influence of which we should be suspicious:

> Whatever they say, dialogue is Vatican licensed, and it is a mine which is powered and installed in our country by America.... And the fruits of this dialogue are poisoning our people (Karaca 2005).

Emin Koc also writes articles frequently defaming Fethullah Gülen in the same *Yeni Mesaj* newspaper. But he goes further to call members of the Hizmet Movement "Christian":

> The love that raises Christian Nur students: These dialogists are playing a "Crusader's Theater" in the disguise of Muslim and call it service, even this should be enough to scare our nation (E. Koc 2005).

In another article, he writes:

> Until this day they [Hizmet Movement (HM)] put their heads to priest's door [Turkish proverb for hoping for help]. They [HM] have appealed to priests and rabbis. They [HM] have embraced them in iftars, Ramadan and even in eids. For priests and rabbis, they [HM] said "these are nice, righteous." They [HM] kissed Pope's hand and said to him "Excellency." They [HM] said "dialogue, world peace, cooperation of civilizations" they hugged priests and rabbis, and begged help from them. They [HM] took Turkish youth to churches.....They [HM] have played with Turkish nation's identity, honor, and civilization, and

they are still playing with it. Yet, these were not enough for them; they [HM] have opened church homes in Muslim neighborhoods where there is not even a single Christian (E. Koc 2006).

The *Yeni Mesaj* newspaper, with its related magazines and weblogs, is affiliated with the Haydar Bas group. Haydar Bas is the chairman of the Independent Turkey Party, a small nationalist and Islamist political party founded in 2001 that regularly receives far below 1% of the votes in elections. Since 2005, the Haydar Bas group has produced CDs that depict Gülen as a Vatican puppet and distributed them throughout mosques in Turkey.

Although no arrests have been made against the Haydar Bas group, some strong evidence points to possible connections with Ergenekon. Some of its leading figures, including Huseyin Mumtaz Beyazit and Abdullah Agir, the former and current vice chairmen of the Independent Turkey Party respectively, are retired army officers. Most of these retired officers were members of Special Forces (paramilitary) when they were active. And according to documents of the latest "military plot to destroy the ruling AK Party and the faith-based Gülen movement," Abdullah Agar is Ergenekon's contact person, leading its activities within the Independent Turkey Party.

Ahmet Akgul and the Milli Cozum Group

Ahmet Akgul and the *Milli Cozum* magazine have published a number of articles generally defaming Gülen as a hypocrite, a Zionist/American agent, and a partner of the Vatican. The *"Milli Cozum* research team" prepared a Fethullah Gülen File, in which they state:

> In the mid-1970's....Fethullah Gülen approached the Masonic powers and established a relationship with Zionist groups who are ruling the world and are behind many dark operations. Because of these connections, Gülen, who does not have any official statue or even a degree, has been able to meet with the Pope and negotiate with politicians.
>
> At first glance, though, it looks like without any official position and education, Gülen has established a large network and been revered for his own efforts (or even miracles according to some claims)... in fact he is presented as such by certain circles [Masonic and Zionist circles]. In reality, he [Gülen] is a tool of this "global gang" of imperialist Zionist capital. He is a figurant who has been played as a hero. It is also revealed by witnesses and official documents that he [Gülen] is not the boss but only a tool (Milli Cozum Research Team 2004).

According to *Milli Cozum*, America's project of "moderate Islam" is even more dangerous than its nuclear weapons, for it allows America to change Islam's genetics (Oguzhan Cildir 2007). The Hizmet Movement, along with the Justice and Development Party and the Deaprtment of Religious Affairs, is complicit in this Zionist crusade by allowing the influence of "moderate Islam and interfaith dialogue" to spread unchecked.

In his writing, Akgul insists on refering to Fethullah Gülen as "Fetullah," stating:

> Today, Fetullah Gülen and his close circle have become fitne (sedition) of infidels and Zionist oppressors. The Fetullahist group's lie of "moderate Islam" is the "catalyst" used by Zionist groups to take Turkey into their own hands. This is why we call him "Fetullah" instead of "Fethullah." Because:
>
> > Fethullah: Door of victory and goodness opened by God.
> > Fet-ullah: God's tool to destroy or scatter something from deep.
>
> So "Fetullah" means catalyst in Arabic. It is an interesting and meaningful coincidence (A. Akgul 2010).

Like other Turkish maligners of Fethullah Gülen, the *Milli Cozum* magazine is also anti-Semitic and anti-Christian. In order to discredit Prime Minister Erdogan, they claim that he is Greek on his father's side and Georgian Jewish on his mother's (Milli Cozum 2010).

Ahmet Akgul had been a member of Necmettin Erbakan's *Milli Gorus* (National View)[7] movement for a long time. He had written in newspapers and magazines affiliated with *Milli Gorus* and published books in that context. But by the beginning of 2000, Akgul had begun to take a more ultra-nationalist (ulusalci) line, closer to Dogu Perincek than Necmettin Erbakan. This change in Akgul's views damaged his relation with the *Milli Gorus* group, and after a couple of years, he was expelled from their meetings and events. In some cities, *Milli Gorus* placed advertisements in newspapers insisting that *Milli Cozum* group has nothing to do with the *Milli Gorus*.

In 2004, Akgul established the *Milli Cozum* newspaper with a small group of supporters, where he continues to write. Four years later, Akgul was detained alongside 25 other people because of his connection to the Ergenekon Terrorist Organization, although the charges were later dropped. However, there are still strong suspicions that the *Milli Cozum* group is financed by the Ergenekon Terrorist Organization.

6.2. ENGLISH

Articles defaming Fethullah Gülen that are written for a Turkish audience can come from opposite sides of the ideological spectrum. But in English, the defamatory articles are written by very ideologically homogenous groups. Most of the English authors condemning Gülen and the Hizmet Movement are fringe radicals, with xenophobic and even racist assumptions coloring their attacks. The dataset includes 88 English articles, 80 of which (or 89%) portray Gülen as an Islamist danger who secretly hopes to establish a caliphate or new Ottoman Empire. However, over half of these articles are produced by same small group of people.

Five English sources are primarily responsible for constructing this defamatory picture: the Middle East Forum, the Last Crusade, Act for America, the Outraged Spleen of the Zion, and the Kurdish Aspect. Other articles were mainly appear on weblogs, and posted by different names, sometimes with no names or nick names. In fact, there are only a handful of anti-Gülen articles that cannot be traced back to one of these five groups in some way. In light of this centeralizatoin, it wouldn't be inappropriate to assume that these authors are related somehow to a larger, coordinated defamation campaign.[8] In other words, the vast majority of these defamatory articles are produced by a small, financially-connected group of people. For instance, Stephen Schwartz, executive director of the Center for Islamic Pluralism in Washington, D.C. wrote a defamatory article that was sponsored by Islamist Watch, a project of the Middle East Forum. So although Schwartz does not work directly for the Middle East Forum, his article was nevertheless sponsored by them.

6.2.1. Middle East Forum

In total, 10 out of 80 articles depicting Gülen as an Islamist threat have been written by authors affiliated with the Middle East Forum. Michael Rubin produced three articles, and Stephen Schwartz wrote an article which has reappeared in three different publications with minor alterations. Hugh Fitzgerald wrote an article which has also been republished several times, and Rachel Sharon-Krespin wrote an article that has been heavily promoted across the internet.

The Middle East Forum, founded in 1990, defines itself as an independent think tank:

> The Forum sees the region [Middle East] — with its profusion of dictatorships, radical ideologies, existential conflicts, exportation of extremism, border disagreements, political violence, and weapons of mass destruction — as a major source of problems for the United States. Accordingly, it urges active measures to protect Americans and their allies.
>
> U.S. interests in the Middle East include fighting radical Islam; working for Palestinian acceptance of Israel; robustly asserting U.S. interests vis-à-vis Saudi Arabia; developing strategies to deal with Iraq and contain Iran; and *monitoring the spread of Islamism in Turkey* (Middle East Forum n.d.).

This last line, *"monitoring the spread of Islamism in Turkey,"* was not part of the forum's original mission statement. It was added recently, and a glance at the list of published articles on the Forum's website clearly shows that *"monitoring the spread of Islamism in Turkey"* has lately become the main focus of the forum. Daniel Pipes, the founder and the director, has never written about Gülen or the Hizmet Movement, but his forum is leading the anti-Gülen campaign. And Pipes and the MEF are well known names among American scholars of the Middle East, not because of their academic work, but because of their history of anti-Islamic defamation.

In 2002, a website established by the MEF called Campus Watch singled out eight professors for their views on Palestine and Islam who were allegedly exposing their students to "dangerous rhetoric." In protest of what they feared could become a McCarthyesque witchhunt, about 100 professors from across the country asked Campus Watch to be added to this list (Schevitz 2002). Prof. Joel Beinin, professor of Middle East History at Stanford University and the President of the Middle East Studies Association (MESA) of North America, was one of those singled out by Campus Watch's "black list." In a response to Campus Watch's defamation campaign, Beinin wrote:

> Another effort to police dissent is focused on those who teach Middle East studies on college campuses. Middle East Forum, a think tank run by Daniel Pipes and supportive of the Israeli right wing, has established a Campus Watch website. After failing in his own pursuit of an academic career, Pipes has evidently decided to take revenge on the scholarly community that rejected him.
>
> Campus Watch seeks to "monitor and gather information on professors who fan the flames of disinformation, incitement, and ignorance." Campus Watch does not care to ask whether scholars who study the Middle East might actually know something that would lead them to think that the world is not simply divided between the forces of good (us) and the forces of evil (them) (Beinin 2002).

In general, Daniel Pipes has a distinctive place in the American history of anti-Muslim bigotry and Islamophobia. He continues to produce materials which advocate a public fear of Muslim people and hatred of the religion of Islam (Islamophobia Watch 2005). Therefore, the anti-Gülen material produced by the Middle East Forum is nothing particularly new; it is simply another way for the MEF to attaack the culture of Islam in general.

On the other hand, it should be said that, compared to the other defamation sources, the authors working at the Middle East Forum are the most professional, and this has unfortunately given their work a certain credibility in the eyes of those who are ready to be suspicious of Islam. It could be said that the defamation of Gülen in English began with varoius authors affiliated with the MEF, such as Michael Rubin or Rachel Sharon-Krespin.

Middle East Forum has even purchased Google advertisements for keywords "Gülen" and "Gülen Movement." From April 27, 2010 to August 9, 2010, whenever someone searched for these terms, Sharon-Krespin's defamatory article at the MEF website appeared on the top or at the right column of the Google's search result as a sponsored link.

Figure 6.1. Google Advertisement for the Keyword " fethullah Gülen"

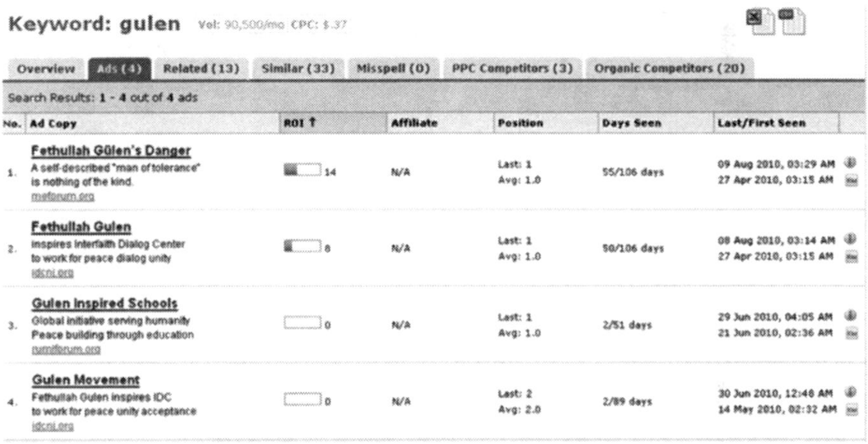

Figure 6.2. Google Advertisement for the Keyword "Gülen"

The images above show which advertisements that have been purchased to appear in the results of a Google search for "Gülen" or "Fethullah Gülen." There are four websites that have paid Google to advertise their link when "Gülen" and "Fethullah Gülen" are entered in the Google search engine, but the second and the fourth are sponsored by the same institution. So only three institutions have purchased advertisements: Middle East Forum, the Interfaith Dialog Center, and the Rumi Forum. Fethullah Gülen is the Honorary President of both the Interfaith Dialog Center (IDC) and the Rumi Forum (RF).

It is understandable that an institution might wish its link to be displayed whenever the name of its honorary president is entered into Google's search engine, but it is more difficult to grasp why an institution would spend money advertising itself in connection to a name with which it is in no way affiliated. This clearly demonstrates the intentions of the Middle East Forum: they are dedicated to the defamation of Fethullah Gülen and are willing to spend money to achieve this end. The online promotion of Sharon-Krespin's defamatory article also suggests that this article was not written coincidentally, it was written for the purpose of defaming Fethullah Gülen (for more information on this article, see next chapter).

6.2.2. The Last Crusade/Paul Williams: A Defamation Machine

Paul Williams is an interesting figure in this defamation campaign. His articles can be found all over the internet, and he appears to be producing them with remarkable frequency. Emerging on the scene in early 2010, he has already written more anti-Gülen articles in English than anyone else. His logic is often inconsistent and difficult to follow though, for he accuses Gülen and the Hizmet movement of being just about everything.

Paul Williams publishes his articles on the "Last Crusade" website, and they often reappear with minor changes on the "Family Security Matters" website. Both of these sites, especially the "Last Crusade," represent an extremely marginal point of view:

> The Last Crusade has emerged from a dark hole within the web to sound again the trumpet for all true believers to engage in a holy war against the pervasive forces of secular humanism (including mainline Christianity), godless socialism, anti-Americanism, and above all, radical Islam (Williams, The Last Crusade 2010).

Williams (2010) is the one who claims that Gülen is training an armed militia at his compound in Pennsylvania. He allegedly lives in a fortress protected by armed guards and helicopters. According to Williams, Gülen works with the CIA and CIA uses Gülen and his money comes from illict drug trafficking but he is secretly trying to establish a caliphate and resurrect the Ottoman Empire. His accusations are imaginative, to say the least:

> These guys use fully automatic weapons – AK-47s – for target practice," one local businessman says. "We called the FBI but nothing has been done to stop them." The Muslims have been here for years," another resident says. "They've been engaged in training for guerilla warfare." The Muslims in question are Turks who occupy a 45-acre compound that is owned and operated by Fethullah Gülen (Williams 2010).

And in another article, Williams writes:

> He [Gülen] also allegedly operates compounds to train jihadis in the tactics of guerilla warfare. This individual has amassed a fortune – – over $30 billion – – for the creation of a universal caliphate. The Saylorsburg property consists of a massive chalet surrounded by numerous out buildings, including recreational centers, dormitories, cabins for visiting foreign dignitaries, a helicopter pad, and firing ranges. Neighbors complain of the incessant sounds of gunfire – – including the rat-tat-tat of fully automatic weapons – – coming the compound and the low flying helicopter that circles the area in search of all intruders. The FBI has been called to the scene, the neighbors say, but no action has been taken to end the illegal activity. Sentries stand guard at the gates to the estate to turn away all curiosity seekers (Williams 2010).

Sometimes Gülen is backed by the CIA, sometimes he is funded by drug trafficking. In his suspicion,Paul Williams has concocted a wildly contradictory account:

> During the Clinton administration, the CIA began to fund the Gülen and his movement with millions derived from drug trafficking – including the revenues amassed by Turkish underworld figures (bubas) from the flow of heroin from Afghanistan through northern Iran to Turkey.
> With the money, Gülen established radical madrassahs (Islamic schools) and cemaats (Muslim communities) throughout the Uzbekistan, Azerbaijan, Kazakhstan, Turkmenistan and newly-formed Russian republics in order to gain control of the vast oil and natural gas reserves of these developing countries.
> The movement grew to attract more than six million Muslim adherents, who supported Gülen's attempt to restore the Ottoman Empire and to establish a universal caliphate (Williams 2010).

After the Williams' artice, Pocono Record Writer, Dan Berrett visited the retreat center where Gülen lives. Berrett spoke to security officers and neighbors living in the neighborhood, and states:

> None of the neighbors with whom the Pocono Record spoke said they had ever heard or seen what Williams described...'You couldn't meet a nicer bunch of people,' said Howard Beers Jr., a Ross Township supervisor who lives next door and enters the property six or seven days a week, often unannounced and not through the front gate, to do construction work. 'If anyone would walk in on something, it would be me,' Beers said. 'As long as I have ever been there, I have never, ever, seen a gun or heard a shot. All this stuff is totally, totally unfounded.' Efforts to reach Williams through the Web site and his blog were unsuccessful (Berrett 2010).

"Act for America," "The Outraged Spleen of the Zion," docstalk.blogspot. com, freedomwatch.com, Gülenwatch.blogspot.com, and other similar weblogs are all of a similar nature. In fact, these weblogs typically do not produce new articles; they simply repost exiting articles produced either by "Last Crusade" or the Middle East Forum. In other words, they are simply used to "spread the word," increasing the circulation of defamatory anti-Gülen (and anti-Islam more generally) articles on the web.

Unfortunately, Paul Williams has a reputation for making baseless and defamatory claims; there is a lawsuit filed against him in the Ontario Superior Court for this very reason. In 2006, Paul Williams wrote a book in which he claimed that a lack of security at McMaster University's nuclear reactor, coupled with the school's abundance of Egyptian-born professors, is enabling al-Qaeda to plot an "American Hiroshima": the planned detonation of nuclear bombs in U.S. cities. The university's lawsuit says that the allegations are false and defamatory, claiming more than two million dollars in damages. Peter Downard, a Toronto lawyer representing McMaster University, states that "the notion that McMaster is then a haven for terrorism because there are people on faculty from Egypt is not only logically offensive, it smacks of racism" (National Post, 2007).

6.2.3. Kurdish Aspect: Aland Mizell

Beyond the echochamber of blogs reposting articles from Paul Williams and the MEF, there is another distinctive group contributing to the defamation of Gülen in English. This group presents itself as a Kurdish group and publishes articles at "Kurdish Media," "Kurdish Aspects," and rastibini. blogspot.com. Aland Mizell is the primary author of this group, writing at kurdishmedia.com, and kurdishaspects.com. Although these websites are most likely not a part of a Gülen defamation campaign, the contributions of Aland Mizell systematically are.

Aland Mizell is the president of Minority Care International, a "non-profit corporation organized exclusively for charitable purposes and designed to carry out its activities in the following areas: Research and Policy Development Survey community resources and needs." Based on its name and mission statement, Minority Care International sounds like a global service organization, but in actuality, it is located exclusively in the Philippines and seems to have only one member: Aland Mizell.

In some articles, he is presented as Dr. Mizell or Professor Mizell and said to be associated with the University of Texas at Dallas. However, the University of Texas at Dallas does not have any faculty by the name of Dr. Aland Mizell. Aland Mizell did attend the University of Texas at Dallas as a PhD student at the department of Political Science and Political Economy, but he failed the doctoral qualification exam that would have awarded him a PhD.

Of course, no one can be discredited simply because they do not have a PhD degree, or even any formal education. But the problem in this case is that Aland Mizell presents himself as a doctor or professor in order to deceive. Like Sharon-Krespin, he uses the title in order to lend credibility to his accusations against Gülen. This is a very common tactic, especially among the more marginal anti-Gülen groups. By using the names of big "international," "global," or "middle eastern" institutions on their websites (some of them are not real at all) and adding titles in front of their names (e.g. Dr., expert), these authors try to present their personal prejudice as expert opinion, which is not at all the case.

In his writings, Aland Mizell continually warns against the resurrection of the new Ottoman Empire, claiming that this is Gülen's "secret project." In one article, he suggests that 10 to 15 years from now, 60% of the United Nations might speak Turkish:

> Gülen himself dreams of ruling the globe; as a result, Gülenists are using religion as the soft power in international relations, remain thirsty for power, and strategize to rule the world, not just Turkey. Because Gülen wants global rule, they are globally engaged politically and consequently they are using a plethora of tactics to change constitutions. Changing the paradigms of international relations, religion-based diplomacy, such as interfaith dialogues, Rumi forums, alliance of civilization, and cultural centers, have emerged. Using an explicit claim that all faiths have common denominators, he really wants to accomplish his goal of world domination but not by common denominators but by his Turkish-brand ideology . I think that one of the Gülen s dreams is to see the majority of the members in the United Nations as his followers and saluting his ideas.

The various English articles defaming Gülen are almost all generate by radical, anti-Islamic, and often racist groups. Paul William defines this mindset on the "Last Crusader" website:

> As crusaders, we remain bloodied, beaten, but unbowed. We shall not lay down our sword until the last jihadi and "Chrislamist" has been vanquished.... Spread the word. We're back – - with a vengeance. No prisoners will be taken. (Williams 2010).

As a matter of fact, Gülen is often perceived as a secondary threat, a harbringer of the greater danger of Islam in general. Among such marginal libelers, everything Islamic is to be attacked:

Islam is NOT a religion of peace. By its nature Islam is radical, it has no shades Most people are simply unaware that Islam is NOT just another religion but a totalitarian political cult-like ideology, which compels its followers into blind obedience, teaches intolerance, brutality and locks all Muslims and non-Muslims in a struggle deriving directly from the 7th century nomadic, predatory, Bedouin culture This blog is designed to show you the dark side of Islam, the REAL Islam that the West does not want you to see. The Islam that Western media refuse to show you.The Islam that is slowly but surely changing the West. You may feel uncomfortable looking at this blog. You should. You will feel anger and disgust that our leaders do not understand Islam when it comes to the motives that drive our enemies to commit suicide for their ideology.

Look at the photos, watch the videos, most of which come right out of the Muslim world, a world that glorifies death and destruction of all that is not Islamic. Understand that elements of Sharia law are creeping into our daily lives under shelter of religious freedom. Listen and learn about the real Islam, then tell your family and friends (Barenakedislam 2010).

6.3. COMMON TACTICS:

Some of these authors (e.g. Aziz Karaca, Emin Koc, Ergun Poyraz, Paul Williams, and Aland Mizell) seem to be dedicated to the single mission of continuously attacking Gülen and the Hizmet Movement. But while the Turkish defamations appear primarily in printed materials, such as books, magazines, and newspapers, the English defamations appear almost exclusively online. This allows for a more rapid spread of misinformation and suspicion in English.

First, a defaming article might appear on an Englsih weblog. Then similar weblogs will link or repost the article, increasing its circulation on the web. After awhile, the same article will reappear if it is a new one.

This means that false information published online in a defamatory article can be repeated and cited by others as if it were a fact. For instance, Sharon Krespin (2009) makes the claim that Gülen controls 25 billion dollars, referencing an Ebaugh and Koc (2008) article as the source of this information. But the Ebaugh and Koc (2008) article does not include any such figure (for more information, see next chapter). In subsequent English articles and weblogs, this "25 billion dollars" appears over and over again, and the Sharon-Krespin (2009) article is now given as the source of the information. In this case, Sharon-Krespin hid false information behind a reference to a credible source until, in the online echochamber of defamatory weblogs, she became the source. Now this false information is presented as if it were the result of Sharon-Krespin's original research.

If circulated frequently enough, false information can become the kind of common knowledge that the public receives without question. So these groups operate several websites and weblogs in both Turkish and English. When new articles appear that defame Gülen or the Hizmet Movement in some way, they are published almost simultaneously on each weblog in an attempt to further reinforce defamatory statements.

NOTES

1. This is ironic, because in the English versions, Gülen is defamed for being all these.

2. Even this change in Cetinkaya's writings, show that there is a strategic change in Gülen's defamation. Cetinkaya who claimed continuesly that Gülen is trying to establish an Islamic state in Turkey, changed his claims in last decade.

3. It is also interesting and impossible for Sharon-Krespin, who is a Turkish Jew, not to know that Gülen is accused for working Israel and even being a crypto Jew in these Turkish articles, yet she accuses Gülen for being anti-Semitic, of course in English version articles.

4. JITEM (Gendarmerie Intelligence Organization) is Ergenekon's military wing and a key organization of the Turkish Army in the Ergenekon Case. Though its existence has been denied by the army officers, this organization has been accused of having illegal operations, including thousands of murders, kidnappings, drug trafficking, especially in the Southeast Kurdish region of Turkey. While it is said that the organization was founded to fight against the PKK terrorists, it is turned out to be an illegal organization itself, controlled by the army officers.

5. Necip Hablemitoglu was a Turkish academician and journalist who was very much in line with the Aydinlik group. He was found dead in his car in 2002. At the time, his murder was blamed on Islamic radicals. But now, the Ergenekon case has shown it to be an operation of the Ergenekon Terrorist Organization.

6. Gülen Movement is intentionally often referred as "Beyond Atlantic- Okyanus Otesi" by these groups in order to emphasize Gülen's involvement with America.

7. Milli Gorus movement is a religio-political movement and a series of Islamist parties inspired by Necmettin Erbakan. Milli Gorus movement or group was started and headed by Turkish politician Necmettin Erbakan. Erbakan advocated that progress, development, and independence would be possible by implication of Islamic morals. He also served as the Prime Minister of Turkey between 1996 and 1997, until he was forced to step down by the military.

8. Recent report published by the Center for American Progress titled "The Roots of the Islamophobia Network in America," which shows that these groups are in fact related and work in campaign manner with millions of dollars budgets. For more information see CAP report at http://www.americanprogress.org/issues/2011/08/pdf/islamophobia.pdf

Chapter 7

An Example: Fethullah Gülen's Grand Ambition

An Example of Biased, Misleading, Mispresented, and Miscalculated Article

One of the most cited articles of the English defamations against Gülen was written by Rachel Sharon-Krespin in the winter of 2009. Titled "Fethullah Gülen's Grand Ambition: Turkey's Islamist Danger," this article was published by Middle East Quarterly, an initiative of the Middle East Forum.

This article is unique in many ways. Unlike other defamatory articles, it is written semi-academically, and the author is portrayed as an objective expert on the issue. As a sort of "mother article," it provided false information as it were fact, allowing many subsequent authors to disguise their own misinformation as academic research by referencing Sharon-Krespin. The Middle East Forum even purchased Google advertisements for this article, as mentioned in the previous chapter.

Anti-Gülen articles written in English can be divided into two categories: "before Sharon-Krespin" and "after Sharon-Krespin." The article was first published in the Winter-2009 edition of the Middle East Quarterly. After this, the number of English defamations skyrocketed, as the graph clearly demonstrates.

Until Sharon-Krespin, only a few anti-Gülen articles were published each year. But in the second half of 2009, when Sharon-Krespin published her article, the total increased to 30 articles.

Outside of presenting some (questionable) data and including a bibliography, the article has little in common with an academic paper written by an expert. It was first brought to my attention by a colleague of mine because of Sharon-Krespin's citation of an article I had co-authored with Helen Rose Ebaugh. Sharon-Krespin writes:

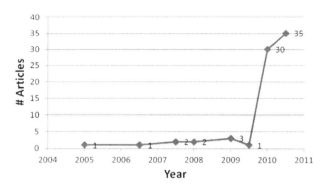

Figure 7.1. Timeline of English Defaming Articles

He [Fethullah Gülen] is a financial heavyweight, controlling an unregulated and opaque budget estimated at $25 billion. (p56)

Sharon-Krespin cites our article as the source of the above information, referencing it in the footnotes as: Helen Rose Ebaugh and Dogan Koç, "Funding Fethullah Gülen-Inspired Good Works: Demonstrating and Generating Commitment to the Movement," (fGülen.com, Oct. 27, 2007). From this, it would appear that Ebaugh and Koç (2007) was the original source of the financial statistic, but her statement misquotes what we presented in the article.

First, I will correct the misperception arising from this use of my own research (Ebaugh and Koç 2007), and then investigate other sources used by Sharon-Krespin (2009) to see if they are used in a similarly misleading manner. Finally, I will address some of the contradictory data that Sharon-Krespin presents.

The article in which this $25 billion statistic can allegedly be found, "Funding Fethullah Gülen-Inspired Good Works: Demonstrating and Generating Commitment to the Movement," was originally a conference paper that Ebaugh and I presented at the London School of Economics during the *Muslim World in Transition: Contributions of the Fethullah Gülen Movement* conference in October, 2007. The article examines the mechanisms used to finance Fethullah Gülen-inspired projects, based on interviews with Turkish business leaders who constitute much of the movement's financial infrastructure. In addition, the paper presents data from one local Gülen-inspired organization in Houston, Texas, that collects thousands of dollars annually from local members, most of them students (Ebaugh and Koç 2007). We framed our essentially sociological analysis in terms of organizational theories of commitment. Beginning with Kanter (1972;1977) and including subsequent major figures in the organizational field (e.g. Reichers 1985; Meyer and Allen 1991; Hall 2002; Scott 2003), scholars have demonstrated a positive correlation between sacrifices asked of members or participants and the degree of their commitment to the goals of an organization. From this perspective, our paper argues that the financial contributions made by participants in the Hizmet Movement both demonstrate and generate commitment to the ideals espoused by Fethullah Gülen.

The Ebaugh and Koç (2007) article defines the Hizmet Movement as a civic movement that arose in Turkey in the late 1960s, initially composed of a loose network of individuals inspired by M. Fethullah Gülen. While our article (Ebaugh and Koç 2007) accepts Woodhall's (2005) statement that the Fethullah Gülen-inspired projects number in the thousands, span international borders, and are costly in terms of human and financial capital, we never estimate the financial amount of contributions. Therefore, the $25 billion that Sharon-Krespin (2009) reports, citing our paper, has no basis in the paper itself or in the data we collected. Where Sharon-Krespin obtains the $25 billion figure remains unknown.

As a matter of fact, when we presented the paper at the London School of Economics, a member of the audience asked after our presentation if we could estimate the financial worth of the movement. We indicated that we could not and that it was not in the scope of our paper to do so. In a later article (Koç 2008), I argued that, since Fethullah Gülen-inspired projects are always locally based and embedded in local circles of supporters, a study of the financial resources of the Hizmet Movement as a whole would require a tally of the resources of all these projects all over the world. Since such research has not occurred, it is impossible for Sharon-Krespin (2009) to state an exact figure for the total resources of Fethullah Gülen-inspired projects.

Apart from encouraging people to donate money, Fethullah Gülen himself has remained distant from any financial involvement. Instead, he has encouraged those who sponsor projects to oversee the use of contributions themselves (Aslandogan and Cetin 2006). During our interviews, one businessman supportive of the movement stated:

> Every school has its own independent accounting system and accountants who manage the budget and financial books. They are all accountable to the local and state authorities, as well as to the trust's sponsors. The local sponsors are knowledgeable about the status of the ongoing projects at any given time, for they are personally responsible for many of them, either as construction contractors, accountants, serving on the board of directors, teachers, principals, etc. It is quite easy, therefore, for them to monitor how the donations are used, thereby achieving transparency in financial issues (Ebaugh and Koç 2007).

Another supporter explained,

> First of all, I want you to know that people in the Hizmet Movement have
> gained the trust of people in every strata of life. People who support the ac-
> tivities of this movement do not worry about whether the support reached its
> destination, they don't chase it. However, if we want to look at it, all kinds of
> information is available in every activity, we can be sure by looking at them
> (Ebaugh and Koç 2007, 544).

In our article, we conclude that:

> Based on the scant literature that exists on the funding of Fethullah Gülen-in-
> spired projects and our own interviews conducted with members of the Fethul-
> lah Gülen Movement both in Turkey and in Houston, Texas, it is evident that
> the money behind the movement is provided by millions of people the world
> over who are committed to the ideas and ideals promoted by Fethullah Gülen
> (Ebaugh and Koç 2007 p. 550).

In light of the errors contained in the Sharon-Krespin article regarding our
paper, one wonders if Sharon-Krespin actually read the article at all. Perhaps
it was simply used as a reference since it contained the words "Funding" and
"Fethullah Gülen" in its title.

7.1. ISSUES REGARDING THE REFERENCES IN SHARON-KRESPIN (2009)

Although, Sharon-Krespin's article has been presented as an academic paper,
it lacks the credible references that would distinguish is as a truly objective
analysis. This is not to suggest that only academic or scientific resources
should be used in academic articles, but there must be criteria by which to
distinguish academic sources from newspaper or weblog articles, which are
not subject to the same accountability. Since Sharon-Krespin (2009) did not
conduct any empirical study or theoretical analysis, her argument depends
primarily on the sources she selects. It is then essential to evaluate these
sources in order to assess the accuracy of her resulting claims. The following table classifies the types of sources referenced by Sharon-Krespin in the
endnotes of her article. (For more details see Sharon-Krespin (2009) endnote
section.)

Before even examining the credibility of the individual sources cited by
Sharon-Krespin (2009), it is necessary to point out that 56.9% are newspaper articles, 27.8% are TV programs, and 4.2% are internet articles. Only
6.9% of the sources are conference or journal articles, and only 4.2% are

Table 7.1. Classification of the Resources According to Source of Information in Sharon-Krespin (2009)

	News Paper Articles	TV Programs	Internet Blog Articles	Conference/ Journal Articles	Books	TOTAL
# of Articles	41	20	3	5	3	72
Percentage in total	56.9%	27.8%	4.2%	6.9%	4.2%	100%

book references. In other words, almost 90% (the combination of newspaper articles, TV programs, and internet blog articles) of the sources used by Sharon-Krespin in the 2009 article are subject to no academic or scientific control for credibility.

For instance, the main references shaping the structure and tone of the Sharon-Krespin (2009) article are taken from non-credible, marginal sources. Sharon-Krespin refers five different times to an interview with Yanarda (or 6.9% of the total number of sources). Yanarda was taken into custody by the Turkish police on October 27, 2008 because of his connection with the Ergenekon Terrorist Organization (ETO) (Taraf 2008). Yanarda was accused because of his connections to a high-ranking ETO member, Tuncay Ozkan, who had also been arrested (Çoban and Turk 2008). Tuncay Ozkan was also the owner of a TV network (Kanal Türk) on which Yanarda gave his interview. Sharon-Krespin also references an interview with Adil Serdar Saçan who was arrested for similar connections to the ETO. This interview, not surprisingly, aired on the Kanal Türk network as well. The interview with Nurettin Veren that Sharon-Krespin quotes several times comes from the same TV network, and the various newspapers and blog articles that appear as references are from similarly non-academic sources, primarily Gülen's Turkish defamers.

Most interesting of all, these sources usually present a picture of Gülen that is the opposite of what Sharon-Krespin asserts. As previous sections have demonstrated, these Turkish articles tend to portray Gülen as an American, Zionist, or Vatican agent. But Sharon-Krespin tries to use these same Turkish articles to depict Gülen as a "shadowy figure who is turning Turkey away from the US and towards Russia and Iran." She claims that Gülen has reorinted Turkish policy in the Middle East away from sympathy with Israel and towards Hamas, Hezbollah, and Syria.

It is ironic that she makes these claims using sources which say almost exactly the opposite. For instance, Merdan Yanardağ and Nurettin Veren were both used as sources in Sharon-Krespin's article. Merdan Yanardağ has written several books defaming Gülen, one of which was an interview with

Nurettin Veren. Here, Yanardağ claims that both the Gülen Movement and the AKP (Justice and Development Party) are controlled by the United States, yet Sharon-Krespin uses these authors to defend her claim that Gülen is leading Turkey away from the US and the West.

7.2. DATA MANIPULATION

Not only does Sharon-Krespin (2009) use questionable references, but she often fails to give references for very important information. And in some cases, she miscalculates and misleads using distorted data. For instance, her article states:

> Today, Turkey has over 85,000 active mosques, one for every 350 citizens—compared to one hospital for every 60,000 citizens—the highest number per capita in the world, and, with 90,000 imams, more imams than doctors or teachers. It has thousands of madrasa-like Imam-Hatip schools and about four thousand more official state-run Qur'an courses, not counting the unofficial Qur'an schools, which may expand the total number tenfold. (p. 55)

No reference is given to justify this statistic (85,000 active mosques, one for every 350 citizens), and so the reader cannot verify the accuracy of the number. Ergener (2002) estimated that the total number of mosques in Turkey was 73,500, with approximately 1,500 mosques built each year. Assuming Ergener's 2002 measure is accurate, after seven years, Sharon-Krespin's (2009) claim of 85,000 mosques would be accurate. However, Sharon-Krespin (2009) also claims that this represents one mosque for every 350 citizens. According to the CIA World Factbook (2009), Turkey's estimated population is 76,805,524. Using simple arithmetic, this works out to one mosque for every 903 people (76,805,524÷85,000). According to the numbers provided by Sharon-Krespin, there is one mosque for every 903 citizens, not every 350 as she claims. In her article, the numbers have been intentionally exaggerated in order to depict Turkey as a hyper-religious country where mosques are more valued than hospitals.

Sharon-Krespin (2009) blames the Justice and Development Party (AKP) and Fethullah Gülen for the transformation of the "fundamental secular and democratic identity" of Turkey, turning it "away from sympathy toward Israel and much more toward friendship with Hamas, Hezbollah, and Syria. Anti-American, anti-Christian, and anti-Semitic sentiments have increased." She implies that Fethullah Gülen and the AKP have increased the number of mosques in Turkey, and they are changing the social fabric of the country by doing so. But the AKP was founded in August 14, 2001 and won the

Turkish election in November 2002. So Ergener's 2002 estimate of 73,500 represents the number of mosques in existence before the AKP government came into office. And the estimated rate of 1,500 mosques being built every year would have been in place even before the AKP took office. If Ergener's (2002) data is accurate, 10,500 (7 multiplied by 1,500) new mosques would have been added to the total number (73,500) in the seven years of AKP governance, putting the total number of mosques in 2009 at 84,000. According to the CIA World Factbook (2003), the population of Turkey was estimated at 67,308,928 in July 2002. This would mean one mosque for every 915 (67,308,928÷73,500) Turksih citizens before the AKP party had even been established. And when we compare the data from 2009 and 2002, we see that there are only 12 (915–903) fewer people for each mosque. This is hardly a change significant enough to warrant the alarmist tone of Sharon-Krespin's article.

In the same paragraph, Sharon-Krespin (2009) also states (again without any source) that there is one hospital for every 60,000 citizens in Turkey. The implication is that while Turkey is full of mosques (here the miscalculation has already been demonstrated), people suffer from lack of health care.

First of all, in health data analysis, it is illogical to measure the number of hospitals per person. The size and capacities of hospitals may differ greatly, so such data is misleading and ultimately useless. For instance, if there are 10 hospitals in Region A, each with a bed-capacity of 1000 in a population of 1,000,000, we can conclude that there is one hospital for every 100,000 people. However, we can also conclude that there is one hospital bed for every 1000 people.

On the other hand, if there are 20 hospitals in Region B, each with a bed-capacity of 100 in a population of 1,000,000, we can conclude that there is one hospital for every 50,000 people. But there is only one bed for every 500 people. In terms of number of hospitals per person, Region B is better served than Region A by a factor of two. But in terms of number of people per hospital bed, Region A is better served than Region B by a factor of five, and this measure more accurately depicts the accessibility of health-care in the two regions. This is why organizations such as the World Health Organization (WHO) and the United Nations (UN) have made the number of "Hospital beds per 10,000 people" the standard measurement of health care access. However, Sharon-Krespin (2009) choose to reference the number of hospitals per person so that she could mislead her readers into thinking that there are 171 (60000÷350) times more mosques than hospitals in Turkey.

Sharon-Krespin's health data misleadingly suggests that access to health care in Turkey is drastically below the global average. The following table presents the World Health Organization's (WHO) global data on health care

Table 7.2. The Number of Hospital Beds (per 10,000 people) and the Health Expenditures Ratio with regards to Turkey*

Member State	Hospital beds (per 10 000 population) 2000-2007	General government expenditure on health as % of total expenditure on health			General government expenditure on health as % of total government expenditure		
		2000	2005	▲ increase	2000	2005	▲ increase
Turkey	27	62.9	71.4	8.5	9.8	13.9	4.1
WHO region							
African Region	9	43.7	45.3	1.6	7.6	8.8	1.2
Region of the Americas	24	45.8	46.8	1.0	16.1	18.0	1.9
South-East Asia Region	...	30.1	29.0	-1.1	4.4	4.9	0.5
European Region	63	73.4	74.3	0.9	13.6	14.7	1.1
Eastern Mediterranean Reg	14	44.8	51.4	6.6	6.9	7.2	0.3
Western Pacific Region	33	59.6	56.8	-2.8	3.6	2.8	-0.8
Global	30	56.0	56.0	0.0	9.0	8.3	-0.7

*Data was obtained from the WHO website, and available at http://www.who.int/whosis/whostat/2008/en/index.html

in so that a comparison can be made between health care conditions in Turkey and conditions in other parts of the world.

According to the WHO data, there are 27 hospital beds in Turkey for every 10,000 people, which is below the global average of 30. However, this is a slightly better ratio than the Region of the Americas (24), two times more than the Eastern Mediterranean (14), and close to both the global average (30) and the Western Pacific Region (33), but less than half of the European Region (63). The data for the South-East Asia Region is not available. Considering that the South-East Asia region includes the most populated region in the world, and that health care provision in this region is usually lower than global average, the inclusion of this region would most likely put Turkey well above the global average. Thus, in terms of numbers of hospital beds per population, Turkey does not rank at the top of the list; however, it is much better than most countries in the world. This is the reality of health care provision in Turkey, but Sharon-Krespin has drawn a picture that is totally contradictory to the facts in order to cast blame on the AKP and Fethullah Gülen.

The WHO data also refutes Sharon-Krespin's claims regarding the AKP by allowing for a comparison between 2000 and 2005. Since the AKP became the ruling party in November 2002, WHO data provides an opportunity to analyze if and how health expenditures changed under its authority.

According to the WHO data, general government expenditure on health as a percentage of total expenditures (the ratio of health expenditure by government to total health expenditure - including both private and government sources) in Turkey was 62.9% in 2000. In 2005, this ratio increased by 8.5%, so that 71.4% of all health expenditures came from the government. While the global average of this measure stayed about the same (56.0%), it decreased in the South East-Asia Region (-1.1%) and Western Pacific Region

(-2.8%); it increased slightly in the African Region (1.6%), the Region of the Americas (1.0%) and the European Region (0.9%). The general government expenditure on health as a percentage of total expenditure on health also increased in the Eastern Mediterranean Region more than other regions (6.6%); however, even this increase was lower than Turkey's. In other words, under the AKP government the general Turkish government expenditure on health as a percentage of total expenditure increased more than in any other region. The AKP government spent more on health care than previous Turkish governments, more even than most of the governments in the world.

The data shows just how much the AKP government increased health care expenditure as a percentage of total government expenditure. The general Turkish government expenditure on health as a percentage of total government expenditure in 2000 was 9.8%, and it increased to 13.9% in 2005. In other words, the government's total health expenditures increased by 4.1% even when global expenditures decreased by 0.7%. This would make the Turkish government's increase in health expenditures one of the highest in the world.

To summarize the data: Turkish government spending on health increased by 8.5% under the AKP government (as a function of total spending only on health), which was one of the biggest increases in the world. And while spending on health decreased or only slightly increased in other parts of the world (as a function of overall government spending), in Turkey, it increased by 4.1% from 2002 to 2005. In conclusion, the WHO data shows that health care conditions in Turkey are not as Sharon-Krespin depicts them. Furthermore, even if they were as she describes, the AKP government has spent more on healthcare than most governments in the world and could hardly be blamed for ignoring the health needs of its citizens. In Turkey, it is widely accepted, even among its opponents, that the health system has imporved dramatically under the AKP government.

Sharon-Krespin also misreports data regarding the budget of the Department of Religious Affairs (RA) (Diyanet İşleri Başkanlığı):

The spending of the RA has grown fivefold, from 553 trillion Turkish lira in 2002 (approximately US$325 million) to 2.7 quadrillion lira during the first four-and-a-half years of the AKP government; it has a larger budget than eight other ministries combined (p. 55).

She cites Can Dündar from Milliyet Newspaper and Reha Muhtar from Vatan Newspaper as her sources for the assertion that Turkey spends more on religious affairs than it does on the eight other government ministries combined (see Sharon-Krespin endnote 1 for details regarding the references). Even though Sharon-Krespin does not directly suggest that the

Department of Religious Affairs is a government ministry, by comparing it to eight "other" ministries, she leads her readers to assume as such. Here it is worth pointing out that Religious Affairs (RA) is not a separate ministry but a secretariat under the Prime Minister. Most of the laws and regulations dictating the tasks of Religious Affairs have been the same throughout the history of the Turkish Republic. The AKP has not done much to change about the role of the RA.

Turkey is the 17th largest economy in the world (IMF 2009, World Bank 2008), and one of the fastest growing as well. The expenditures of various government ministries amount to billions of dollars. If Sharon-Krespin's estimate were accurate and Turkey was in fact spending more than this on Religious Affairs, this enormous amount of money would initiate huge debates both in Turkey and in the EU. But such discussion is absent both in Turkey and the EU, simply because the data presented by Sharon-Krespin (2009) is grossly inaccurate.

The source from which Sharon-Krespin derives these budget figures (Milliyet newspaper), paints a very different picture of the budget. Milliyet (2006) presents the 2006 budget for different government ministries (actual numbers), accompanied by a conjectural budget for 2007:

As can be seen clearly, the budget for Religious Affairs was only 0.78% of the total expenditure in 2007. The budget for the Ministry of Defense was 6.3%; the Ministry of Education had 10.4%; and the Ministry of Health had 3.2% of the total expenditure in 2007. The total budgets of these three ministries (Ministries of Defense, Education, and Health) is 25 times larger than the budget for Religious Affairs. One wonders which eight ministries Sharon-Krespin was referring to and where she got her data, since the source that she quotes presents a totally different interpretation of the facts.

Sharon-Krespin's problematic presentation of financial data concludes with the following claim:

> The spending of the RA has grown fivefold, from *553 trillion* Turkish lira in 2002 (approximately *US$325* million) to *2.7 quadrillion* lira during the first four-and-a-half years of the AKP government...

While Sharon-Krespin converts the 2002 data into US Dollars, she neglects to make the same calculation for 2006, exaggerating the difference between the two figures. And when mentioning the "2.7 quadrillion lira," she fails to inform readers that Turkey deleted 6 zeros from its currency at the beginning of 2005. Therefore, it is misleading to compare the old currency to the 2006 currency without any adjustment. But by using old currency measures and failing to convert them to US dollars, Sharon-Krespin bolsters her argument with distorted facts.

Table 7.3. Comparison of Budgets of the Religious Affairs to the Ministries of Defense, Education and Health*

	Religious Affairs (RA)	Ministry of Defense	Ministry of Education	Ministry of Health
2000	268	3,745	3,461	1,14
2001	400	5,414	5,145	1,822
2002	619	7,743	8,043	3,039
2003	862	8,841	10,583	3,674
2004	1,015	9,440	13,016	4,461
2005	1,150	10,282	14,863	6,769
2006	1,373	8,560	15,710	7,814
2007	1,600	13,000	21,355	6,600

Numbers are in million YTL (Turkish Lira, 1 USD= 1,6 YTL)

Percentage of the Budget in Total Expenditure

2000	0.58%	8.10%	7.50%	2.50%
2001	0.50%	6.80%	6.40%	2.30%
2002	0.54%	6.70%	7%	2.60%
2003	0.62%	6.30%	7.60%	2.60%
2004	0.73%	6.80%	9.30%	3.20%
2005	0.80%	7.20%	10.30%	4.70%
2006	0.88%	5.50%	10.10%	5%
2007	0.78%	6.30%	10.40%	3.20%

*Milliyet (2006) indicates that the data is based on the Ministry of Treasury

7.3. SELECTIVE INFORMATION

In her analysis of Fethullah Gülen's intentions, Sharon-Krespin quotes several paragraphs from his speeches in which Fethullah Gülen seems to be encouraging people to secretly organize in order to gain power within a government or institution. Most of these speeches were broadcast in Turkey during a defamation campaign against Fethullah Gülen in 1998. Fethullah Gülen denied the accusations, stating that quotes had been excerpted without any context. Aslandogan (2006) points out:

> A concurrent phenomenon that happened exactly during this period was the passing of important legislation for the regulation of the banking sector and a banking crisis that eventually cost the state treasury the equivalent of nearly 100 billion dollars. The peculiar coincidence of the media campaign against Fethullah Gülen and the banking legislation that was at the national assembly during this campaign was noticed by Turkish intellectuals as well as by Mr. Bülent Ecevit, then the prime minister of Turkey. Ecevit voiced his opinion that the media campaign was intended to divert public attention from important legislation to the detriment of the country. Later revelations and developments over time have unfortunately confirmed the prime minister. (p. 2)

Aslandogan suggests that this defamation campaign was launched against Fethullah Gülen as a smoke-screen to divert public attention from the loss of close to 100 billion dollars at the hands of the financial elite. Aslandogan (2006) also states that the chief attorney for the Ankara National security court, Nuh Mete Yüksel, conducted an investigation into the matter of Gülen's alleged conspiracy:

> It was later revealed that the clips that formed one of the bases of the campaign were excerpted without context and montages were done to leave the impression that Fethullah Gülen was organizing a secret group of government workers to later take over the government. These turned out to be context-free cut and pastes from multiple cassettes that left a completely different impression of Fethullah Gülen's intentions. (p. 4)

Sharon-Krespin quotes the video montages as if they were truly representative speeches, failing to mention the rest of the case. She excerpts her quotes from doctored video clips and therefore has no understanding of the context in which they were originally intended.

Furthermore, she states:

> In 2008, members of the Netherland's Christian Democrat, Labor, and Conservative parties agreed to cut several million euros in government funding for organizations affiliated with "the Turkish imam Fethullah Gülen" and to thoroughly investigate the activities of the Fethullah Gülen group after Erik Jan Zürcher, director of the Amsterdam-based International Institute for Social History, and five former Fethullah Gülen followers who had worked in Fethullah Gülen's ışıkevi told Dutch television that the Fethullah Gülen community was moving step by step to topple the secular order. (p. 59)

A NOVA documentary titled "Kamermeerderheid Eist Onderzoek Naar Turkse Beweging" is the only source given for the information quoted above. This documentary is simply a collection of unsubstantiated claims made against the Hizmet Movement and Fethullah Gülen himself that are similar to the defamations made by marginal groups in Turkey. In fact, Hikmet Çetinkaya of Cumhuriyet newspaper appears several times in the film. Most of the claims in the film are supported by statements from five "former Fethullah Gülen followers." The faces of these five people are obscured and their voices are changed in order to hide their identities. The producers of the film probably thought this was necessary in order to protect them, but it also serves to give an air of subterfuge to the entire piece which makes their claims difficult to factually refute. It may have been done because in reality there are no such "former Fethullah Gülen followers," but only people who were paid to speak as instructed.

On the decision by the Netherland's Christian Democrat, Labor, and Conservative parties to cut funding to the schools, Sharon-Krespin provides no source for this information. If the source is meant to be the aforementioned film or documentary as one assumes, then the statement is again misleading. The film only asks the government of the Netherlands to cut funding after presenting its arguments against Gülen and the Hizmet movement. But there is no corroboration of funding actually being cut. Sharon-Krespin asserts the wishes of this marginal group as if they were facts.

7.4. CONTRADICTIONS AND AMBIGUITIES IN SHARON-KRESPIN (2009)

A series of excerpts from the Sharon-Krespin article reveals the contradiction in her claims regarding the nature of Fethullah Gülen's allegiance (2009):

> Prior to the AKP's rise, Ankara oriented itself toward the United States and Europe. Today, despite the rhetoric of European Union accession, Prime Minister Recep Tayyip Erdoğan has turned Turkey away from Europe and toward Russia and Iran and reoriented Turkish policy in the Middle East away from sympathy toward Israel and much more toward friendship with Hamas, Hezbollah, and Syria. Anti-American, anti-Christian, and anti-Semitic sentiments have increased. (p. 55)

> In October 2007, the British House of Lords feted Fethullah Gülen with a conference in his honor. (p. 57)

> …the Russian government, weary of the movement's activities in majority Muslim regions of the federation, has banned not only the Fethullah Gülen schools but all activities of the entire Nur sect in the country. (p. 59)

And when speaking of Gülen's immigration case, she notes:

> Two former CIA officials, George Fidas and Graham Fuller, and former U.S. ambassador to Turkey Morton Abramowitz also supplied references. (p. 65)

Even though the claim is not made directly, Sharon-Krespin implies (the title of this section is "US Government Support for Fethullah Gülen") that by granting Gülen residency, the US government is backing the Hizment movement and condoning its activities.

Here the contradiction between the two defamatory pictures of Gülen resurfaces in a confusion of allegiance. At the beginning of the article, Sharon-Krespin (2009) attracts the attention of the Western reader by asserting that Turkey is no longer EU–USA oriented but has a growing relationship with Russia and Iran. However, her later quotes indicate that the EU and the USA support Fethullah Gülen, while it is the Russian government that has banned Fethullah Gülen-inspired schools. If the AKP and Fethullah Gülen are trying to pull Turkey towards Russia and Iran and away from the EU and USA, one wonders why Russia is banning its schools (even though this information is also not accurate), why the British House of Lords is organizing a conference in Fethullah Gülen's honor, why CIA agents and US diplomats are providing references for Fethullah Gülen, and why the US government has granted him residency rights.

In conclusion, Sharon-Krespin provides a picture of Turkey and Fethullah Gülen that is based on distortions of factual evidence. Sharon-Krespin's article reminds us yet again how careful we as readers have to be in interpreting the information presented to us, and it provides an unfortunate example of how false conclusions can be drawn from biased, miscalculated, misleading, and misrepresentative data.

Chapter 8

Concluding Remarks

Reviews of various individual articles and the statistical analyses of the data set suggest that the defamation of Fethullah Gülen and the Hizmet Movement is conducted strategically. Gülen is portrayed simultaneously as an Islamic threat, secretly trying to resurrect the Ottoman Empire and Caliphate, and as an American Zionist puppet whose "moderate Islam" threatens to destroy Turkey and subvert the Muslim world. This difference clearly reveals more about the suspicions of different audiences than it does about Gülen. The fear of an Islamic leader secretly trying to resurrect the Ottoman Empire and Caliphate resonates more with English readers, whereas the thought of an American and Zionist puppet destroying resonates with the fears of Turkish readers. It is difficult not to agree with Turker's (2009) claim that:

> One wonders how come these critics can contradict each other this much even though they use the same sources. How come they criticize Gülen for being an American and Zionist puppet (Turkish versions) but at the same time as an Islamic danger who is trying to establish an anti-American, anti-Semitic Islamic state (English versions)?
>
> In fact, it is not that difficult to understand because they are addressing different audiences. It makes more sense to warn Turkish speakers of an American imperialist danger which is supported by Zionists. But, on the other hand, for English speakers, you will find more buyers if you use an Islamic danger argument. However, those who can read both languages will see the hypocrisy therein.

Although, I am able to demonstrate how these defamations are strategically organized, I have left two important matters unaddressed in this book:

(1) How can these claims be refuted or disproved? (2) What motivates these groups to defame Gülen and the Hizmet Movement?

Since these claims are defamatory, it is difficult to furnish enough evidence to counter the dishonesty of false accusations. As common wisdom suggests, proving the non-existince of a claim is much more difficult than proving existence of a claim. How can one prove that Gülen is not "financed by CIA drug trafficking money," as Williams claims, except by demonstrating that there is no evidence at all that would support such an accusation. But that is what characterizes these articles and books as defamatory: they are not concerned with accuracy, they simply wish to damage Gülen's reputation and tarnish the name of the Hizmet movement.

But it is not Gülen's responsibility to prove 'what he is not;' the burden of proof falls on the authors to demonstrate their claims. In other words, Williams must provide convincing evidence that the "CIA supports Gülen with the money they receive from drug trafficking," and Aland Mizell must offer tangible proof that "Gülen is taking over the United Nations." Or as it is claimed in Turkish versions of the defamation articles, Hikmet Cetinkaya must provide evidence demonstrating that "the Gülen Movement is an American project" and Aytunc Altindal must prove that Gülen is an 'in pecture' (secret) cardinal of the Pope. How can Gülen, or anybody else for that matter, deal with these absurd claims except by denying their veracity?

Therefore, I did not try to explain or disprove any of the claims made by these defamation authors. Rather, I tried to show how these claims are strategically selected and targeted according to audinces' sensitivities and priorities.

However, I included a lengthy response to Sharon-Krespin's article in the book in order to show just how facts are distorted and data is manipulated in the supposed "proofs" of these defamatory claims. The Sharon-Krespin article was chosen because of its widespread use as a source among other defamatory pieces. But it was also chosen because it is one of the few defamatory English articles that even attempts to use evidence in support of its claims, even if this evidence is distorted and unreliable.

For instance, Sharon-Krespin's picture of the health system in Turkey can be challenged by WHO (World Health Organization) data; I can consult the calculations and argue that her interpretation of the data is incorrect. However, I don't see any way to prove that a person is not an agent of the CIA or a secret cardinal of the Pope, no matter who that person is.

To answer the second question (What motivates these groups to defame Gülen and the Hizmet Movement?) would be to move beyond the scope of this research. The third section of this book provides speculates somewhat about the motivations of these groups, and I could have provided more information on each of the Turkish defamation authors. But I did not think that would be appropriate within the context of this analysis. These marginal groups have been targeting Gülen for a long time, and so there is plenty of available data outlining their political interests. Furthermore, the ongoing criminal and terror invastigations in Turkey (especially Ergenekon Terrorist Organization case) continue to reveal connections between these groups, suggesting that they are coordinated by Turkey's established ultra-nationalist and ultra-secularist elites. For those in power, the argument goes, the Gülen Movement challenges the statu quo by striving to educate millions of students from the middle and lower classes. However, a comprehensive analysis of these groups and their various affiliations would require an intensive knowledge of Turkish political history. That is not within the scope of this book, and I do not want to lose English readers in a mass of foreign historical details.

Turkish anti-Gülen articles have been around for some time, but English versions have just started to appear recently. Therefore, it is difficult at this point to understand exactly what motivates the groups producing these. However, time will provide more information about these English anti-Gülen groups, and we will learn in time whether or not they are affiliated at all with the authors publishing defamatory articles in Turkey.

The authors mentioned here have continuously tried to discredit the actictivites of the Hizmet Movement in Turkey, but they have failed. The Hizmet Movement has received support from a vast majority of Turkish people, intellectuals, and elected governments across the political spectrum. The movement has been welcomed by the people and leaders of more than one hundred countries.

Due to the importance of the United States in the world and the activities of the Hizmet Movement in the United States, the same groups continue to defame Gülen, now with the assistance of certain local radical groups. But these attacks failed in Turkey, even despite its fragile democratic structure, and it is all the more likely they will fail in the United States. The inclusive character of democracy in the the United States will not be cowed by the accusations of a few marginal groups. However, the defamations do create an atmosphere of suspicion around Gülen and the Hizmet Movement. This is precisely the purpose of the defamatory articles: to manipulate evidence in order to discredit the Hizmet Movement in the minds of those who have no experience with it. And it is the purpose of this book to educate anyone who is interested in the Movement, and present information that they may not be able to reach due to language.

I have no doupt that these marginal groups will not be able to discredit Gülen or the Hizmet Movement in the Western World in general and the United States in particular. However, it is the responsibility of those of us who believe in world peace enough to work for it, to present facts as they are. We give the public the oppournity to challange and question the assumptions of radical and marginal groups.

The Hizmet Movement is a unique cultural phenomenon that cannot be discredited by some marginals and radicals. It is a moderate, peaceful voice in the Muslim World calling for dialogue, understanding, and integration. As the movement continues to reach out the Western World, it will continue to play an important role in the establishment of peace between people of all beliefs. No one, including the radical, and marginal groups of any country (whether Turkey or the United States), has the right to sabotage this peaceful process.

Bibliography

Acik Istihbarat. 2010. http://www.acikistihbarat.com/Haberler.asp?haber=5420 (accessed August 15, 2010).

Acik Istihbarat. "Fethullah Sebekinin Baglantilari." *Acik Istihbarat.* http://www .acikistihbarat.com (accessed August 6, 2010).

Ademoglu, Abdullah. "Defamation of Gulen as a Smoke Screen." *Fethullah Gulen Forum.* April 5, 2010. http://www.fethullahgulenforum.org (accessed August 19, 2010).

Ahmed, Akbar. 2007. *Journey into Islam: The Crisis of Globalization.* Washington, D.C.: Brookings Institution Press.

Agai, Bekim. 2005. "Discoursive and organizational strategies of the Gülen movement." Paper presented at the conferenceon Islam in the Contemporary World: The Fethullah Gülen Movement in Thought and Practice, Rice University, November 12-13, Houston, Texas.

Akgul, Abdullah. "PKK'ya saygi, TSK'ya Saldiri." *Milli Cozum*, September 19, 2009.

Akgul, Ahmed. "Fitnetullah ve Baykal." *Milli Cozum*, May 18, 2010.

Akman, Nuriye 1995. "Interview with Fethullah Gulen" *Nokta*, February 18, pp. 16-18.

Alpay, Sahin. 1996. "Fethullah Gulen". *Milliyet*, November 4.

Altindal, Aytunc. *Vatikan ve Tapınak Şövalyeleri.* Alfa Yayinlari, 2004.

Aras, Bulent and Omer Caha.2000. "Fethullah Gulen and his Liberal "Turkish Islam" Movement " *Middle East Review of International Affairs*, Vol. 4, No. 4.

Aslan, Adnan. 2005. "Interfaith Dialogue in the Context of New Theological Language and Fethullah Gülen." Paper presented at the conferenceon Islam in the Contemporary World: The Fethullah Gülen Movement in Thought and Practice, Rice University, November 12-13, Houston, Texas.

Aslandogan, Y. Alp, "Defation as a Smoke-Screen: A Case in Modern Turkey" in *Islam in the Contemporary World: The Fethullah Gülen Movement in Thought and Practice.* 3-5 November 2006, University of Oklahoma, Norman, OK.

http://www.scribd.com/doc/3932175/Aslandogan-Ya-Defamation-as-a-Smoke -Screen?autodown=pdf(accessed May 26, 2009).

Aslandogan, Yuksel, and Muhammed Cetin. "The Educational Philosophy of Gülen in Thought and Practice." In Muslim Citizens of the Globalized World: Contributions of the Gülen Movement, by Robert Hunt and Yuksel Aslandogan, 31-54. New Jersey: The Light, 2006.

Aydinlik. "Suikastta MOSSAD- Fethullah Hatti." December 22, 2002: 4.

Aytac, Onder, and Emre Uslu. "Ulusalcı-İBDA-C İlişkisi." *Taraf*, June 30, 2008.

Aytac, Onder, and Onder Uslu. "İslamcı Ergenekon: İBDA-C, Hizb-ut Tahrir, Haydari, Hizbullah, Nizam-ı Âlem, Gülen cemaati ve AKP." *Taraf*, September 22, 2008.

Bala, Tevfik. "ILIMLI İSLAM TUZAĞI ." *Milli Cozum*, September 1, 2006.

Barenakedislam. 2010. barenakedislam.wordpress.com/about/.

Beinin, Joel. "Who's Watching the Watchers?" *History News Network*, September 30, 2002.

Bell, Alistair. 1995. "Turkish Islamic Leader Defies Radical Label," *Reuters*, August 7.

Berkes, Niyazi. 1998. *The Development of Secularism in Turkey.* London, England: Routledge.

Biskin, Necmettin. "MASONLUK VE DİNLERARASI DİYALOG İLİŞKİSİ VE SİYONİSTLERİN ERBAKAN ENDİŞESİ." *Milli Cozum*, March 1, 2007.

Borne, M. E. "Ceux qui font ecole a part." *Le Monde De L'Education*, January 22, 2008.

Bozkurt, Abdullah. "Ergenekon Fact vs. Fiction - Unraveling the trial of the century." *Today's Zaman*, April 21, 2010.

Can, Eyüp 1996. *Fethullah Gülen ile Ufuk Turu.* Istanbul, Turkye: A.D.

Cetin, Muhammed. 2005. "Mobilization and Counter-mobilization: The Gülen Movement in Turkey." Paper presented at the conference on Islam in the Contemporary World: The Fethullah Gülen Movement in Thought and Practice, Rice University, November 12-13, Houston, Texas.

Cetin, Muhammed. 2008. "Collective Identity and Action on the Gulen Movement: Implications for the Social Movement Theory" Ph.D. dissertation, School of Education, Human Sciences and Law of the University of Derby, Derby, UK.

Cetinkaya, Hikmet. *Amerikan Mızıkacıları.* Istanbul: Cumhuriyet Kitaplari, 2009.

———. *Din Baron'un Kazlari.* Istanbul: Gunizi Yayincilik, 2006.

———. *Fethullah Gülen ABD ve AKP.* Istanbul: Gunizi Yayincilik, 2007.

———. *Fethullah Gülen'in 40 Yıllık Serüveni.* Istnabul: Gunizi Yayincilik, 2004.

———. *Fethullah Gülen'in 40 Yıllık Serüveni-2nd book.* Istanbul: Gunizi Yayincilik, 2005.

———. *Fethullahçı Gladyo.* Istanbul: Gunizi Yayincilik, 2008.

———. "GÜLEN'İN KUZEY IRAK'TAKİ OKULUNU TUNCAY GÜNEY KURDU." *Birgun Net.* June 29, 2009. http://www.birgun.net/research_index .php?category_code=1246272950&news_code=1246277127&action=read (accessed September 1, 2010).

Cetinkaya, Himket. *Soros'un Çocukları* . Istanbul: Cumhuriyet Kitaplari, 2008.

CIA. CIA *The World Factbook.* March 19, 2003. (accessed May 12, 2009).

———. CIA *The World Factbook.* April 29, 2009. (accessed May 12, 2009).

Chittick, William C.1999. "Introduction to Sufism." Pp 12-35 in *Merton & Sufism: The Untold* Cildir, Oguzhan. "Fethullah mi? Finetullah mi?" *Milli Cozum*, May 2007.

Story, edited by Rob Baker and Gray Henry. Louisville, KY: Fons Vitae.

Çevik, İlnur.2006. Fethullah Gulen Factor in Our Political Scene. Turkish Daily News. 11 May, 2006.

Çoban, Cengiz, and Ümit Turk. "Tuncay Özkan Gözaltında." *Hurriyet*, September 23, 2008.

Deniz, Ahmet. "DOSTU AMERİKA OLANIN POSTU MEZATA ÇIKAR!" *Milli Cozum*, September 1, 2007.

dictionary.com. *Dictionary.* 2010. http://dictionary.reference.com/browse/defamation (accessed August 12, 2010).

Duyar, Dogan. "Ogretmenlere Amerikan Pasaportu." *Aydinlik*, March 1, 1998.

Ebaugh, H.R. and Dogan Koc. 2007. "Funding Gulen-inspired Good Works: Demonstrating and Generating Commitment to the Movement." Pp. 539-552 in the conference proceeding Muslim World in Transition: Contributions of Gulen Movement. London, England: Leeds University Press.

Eickelman, Dale F. 1998. "Inside the Islamic Reformation," *Wilson Quarterly* 22, No. 1.

Eraydin, Osman. "SİYONİST SERMAYENİN 'NGO'LARI VE EMPERYALİZMİN SİVİL LEJYONLARI." *Milli Cozum*, November 1, 2007.

Erdogan, L. 1995. *Küçük Dünyam.* Istanbul, Turkey: Dogan Yayincilik.

Ergener, Rashid. *About Turkey: Geography, Economy, Politics, Religion, and Culture* . Santa Fe: Pilgrims Process, Inc., 2002.

Etzioni, Amitia. 1961. *A Comparative Analysis of Complex Organizations.* New York: Free Press of Glencoe.

Eygi, Mehmet Sevket. 2000a."Turkic World" *Milli Gazete*, 5 May, 2000.

Eygi, Mehmet Sevket. 2000b. "Secret Agreement with Papacy" *Milli Gazate,* 26 May 2000.

Ekmekci, Hakan. "ÖCALAN CUMHURBAŞKANI, FETULLAH DİYANET VE DİYALOG BAKANI! ." *Milli Cozum*, November 24, 2008.

Eygi, Mehmet Sevket. "Secret Agreement with Papacy." *Milli Gorus*, May 26, 2000.

—. "Turkic World." *Milli Gazete*, May 5, 2000.

Eygi, Mehmet Şevket. "Secret Agreement with Papacy." *Milli Gorus*, May 26, 2000.

Filiz, Sahin. "Diyalog"un Temeli Isa Mesih Hristiyanligi." *Aydinlik*, February 11, 2007: 10.

Fitzgerald, Hugh. *Jihadwatch.* 2008. http://jihadwatch.com (accessed August 5, 2010).

Foreign Policy.2008. " World's Top Public Intellectual" July/August.

Goldman, David. "Fethullah Gulen's cave of wonders." *Asia Times.* June 9, 2010. http://atimes.com (accessed August 8, 2010).

Gozubuyuk, Yakup. "KÜRTLEŞMİŞ YAHUDİLERLE İSRAİL İLİŞKİLERİ, PKK-FETULLAHCILIK İŞBİRLİĞİ ." *Milli Cozum*, October 28, 2009.

Gulaltay, Semih Tufan. *Fethullah Musluman mi?*

Gurdogan, Burhan. "The Gulen Movement is a danger spreading from Turkey to the world." *The Comment Factory.* January 30, 2010. http://www.thecommentfactory. com (accessed July 7, 2010).

Gülen, Fethullah. 1995. *Fasildan Fasila 1.* Izmir, Turkey: Nil Yayinevi.

Gulen, Fethullah. 1995. *Prophet Muhammed: The Infinite Light.* London, England: Truestar.

Gülen, Fethullah. 1996. *Towards the Lost Paradise.* London, Turkey: Truestar.

Gülen, Fethullah. 1997. *Understanding and Belief: The Essentials of Islamic Faith.* Izmir, Turkey: Kaynak.

Gülen, Fethullah. 1999. *Key Concepts in the Practice of Sufism.* Fairfax, Virginia: The Fountain.

Gülen, Fethullah. 2000. *Pearls of Wisdom.* Fairfax, Virginia: The Fountain:

Gülen, Fethullah. 2001. "A Comparative Approach to Islam and Democracy." *SAIS Review* XXI, No. 2:133-138

Gülen, Fethullah. 2004a. *Toward a Global Civilization of Love & Tolerance.* New Jersey: The Light Inc.

Gülen, Fethullah. 2004b. *Love and the Essence of Being Human.* Istanbul, Turkey: Journalists and Writers Foundation Publications.

Hankin, Ron.*Navigating the Legal Minefield of Private Investigations: A Career-Saving Guide for Private Investigators, Detectives, And Security Police*: Looseleaf Law Publications, 2008.

Hablemitoglu, Necib. 2000. Yeni Hayat. N.52

Hendrick, Joshua D. 2006. "Global Islam and the Secular Modern World: Transnational Islamic Revivalism and the Movement of Fethullah Gülen, A Comparative Approach." Paper presented at the conference on Islam in the Contemporary World: The Fethullah Gülen Movement in Thought and Practice, Southern Methodist University, March 3-4, Dallas, Texas.

Hermansen, M. 2000. "Understandings of "Community" within the Gülen Movement." Paper presented at the conference on Islam in the Contemporary World: The Fethullah Gülen Movement in Thought and Practice, Rice University, November 12-13, Houston, Texas.

IMF. *World Economy Outlook Database.* IMF, (accessed May 12, 2009).

Kalyoncu, Mehmet. *A Civilian Response to Ethno-Religious Conflict: The Gülen Movement in Southeast Turkey.* New York: The Light, 2008.

Karaca, Aziz. "Bu Yolu Acanlara Lanet Olsun." *Yeni Mesaj,* January 1, 2006.

———. "Diyalog coğrafyamıza döşenen bir mayındır." *Yeni Mesaj,* October 28, 2005.

———. "Diyaloga karşıyız, çünkü...." *Yeni Mesaj,* February 18, 2005.

———. "Diyalogun bir adım sonrası işgaldir." *Yeni Mesaj,* December 22, 2006.

———. "Diyalog meyveleri zehirliyor." *Yeni Mesaj Gazetesi,* March 09, 2005.

———. "Diyaloga karşıyız, çünkü...." *Yeni Mesaj Gazetesi,* February 18, 2005.

———. "Misyonerlik bir iddia mı gerçek mi?" *Yeni Mesaj*, February 8, 2005.

———. "Vatikan tarafından sulanan diyalog meyveleri." *Yeni Mesaj*, May 20, 2005.

Internet Haber. *Konya'da Ergenekon ağı.* July 23, 2008. http://www.internethaber. com/konyada-ergenekon-agi-149975h.htm (accessed August 15, 2010).

Islamophobia Watch. *Islamophobia Watch.* 2005. http://www.islamophobia-watch. com/about-us/ (accessed August 22, 2010).

Kalyoncu, Mehmet. 2008. A Civilian Response to Ethno-Religious Conflict: The Gulen Movement in Southeast Turkey. The Light: New York

Kim, Heon. 2005. "F. Gülen and Sufism: A Contemporary Manifestation of Sufism." Paper presented at the conferenceon Islam in the Contemporary World: The Fethullah Gülen Movement in Thought and Practice, Rice University, November 12-13, Houston, Texas.

Kizilkan, Nail. "RECEP ERDOĞAN OF THE USA AND THE REINS OF BARACK OBAMA ." *Milli Cozum*, December 29, 2008.

Kristianasen, Wendy. 1997. "New Faces of Islam." *Le Monde Diplomatique,* July. Retrieved October 12, 2006 (http://mondediplo.com/1997/07/turkey).

Koc, Dogan. "Generating an Understanding of Financial Resources in the Gülen Movement: Kimse Yok mu Solidarity and Aid Foundation." Islam in the Age of Global Challenges: Alternative Perspectives of the Gülen Movement. Washington, D.C.: Rumi Forum Press, 2008. 435-454.

Koc, Dogan. ""Fethullah Gülen's Grand Ambition": A Biased, Selective, Misleading, Misrepresentative and Miscalculated Article." *Fethullah Gulen Forum.* January 29, 2010. http://www.fethullahgulenforum.org (accessed August 5, 2010).

Koc, Dogan. 2006. "Gulen's Understanding of Sufism." Paper presented conferenceon Islam in the Contemporary World: The Fethullah Gülen Movement in Thought and Practice, University of Oklahoma, November 4-5, Norman, Oklahoma.

Koc, Emin. "BOP işgalleri öncesi toplum mühendisliği." *Yeni Mesaj*, April 24, 2006.

———. "Diyalogcu nurcunun "İncilli meali"nden BOP'un "Furkan'ül Hakk"ına." *Yeni Mesaj*, March 14, 2006.

———. "Diyalogcu nurcunun "İncilli meali"nden BOP'un "Furkan'ül Hakk"ına." *Yeni Mesaj*, MArch 14, 2006.

———. "Gulen, RTE ve Avanesi ADL Hizmetcisi." *Yeni Mesaj*, May 10, 2005.

———. "Hiristiyan Nur Talebeleri." *Yeni Mesaj*, December 12, 2005.

———. "Rahiplerin örümcek ağları." *Yeni Mesaj*, January 26, 2005.

Koc, M. Emin. "Papazın ölüsünden medet umanlar." *Yeni Mesaj*, February 10, 2006.

Kuru, Ahmet. 2003. "Fethullah Gulen's Search for a Middle Way Between Modernity and Muslim Tradition." Pp. 123-142 in *Turkish Islam and the Secular State: The Gülen Movement*, edited by Hakan Yavuz, John Espesito. New York: Syracuse University Press.

Mardin, Serif. 1989. *Religion and Social Change in Modern Turkey: The Case of Bediuzzaman Said Nursi.* Albany: State University of New York.

Mater, Nadire. 1995. "Rise of Secular Priest Seen as a Threat by Islamicists." *Inter Press Service*, February 22.

Michel, Thomas.2005. "Sufism and Modernity in the Thought of Fethullah Gulen." *Muslim World* 95, No 3.

Middle East Forum. *Middle East Forum.* http://www.meforum.org/about.php (accessed August 17, 2010).

Milli Cozum. "Cover Page." *Milli Cozum*, October 2010.

Milli Cozum Research Team. "Fethullah Gulen Dosyasi." *Milli Cozum.* January 1, 2004. http://www.millicozum.com/mc/ARALIK-2004/fetullah-gulen-dosyasi.html (accessed August 12, 2010).

Milli Gorus Research Team. "Fethullah Gulen Dosyasi." *Milli Gorus*, December 1, 2004.

Milliyet. *Milliyet.* December 26, 2006. http://www.milliyet.com.tr/2006/12/27/ekonomi/eko01.html (accessed May 17, 2009).

Mizell, Aland. "Does terrorism help Gülen's Muslim missionaries? A first class revolution from the bottom up ." *Kurdish Media.* August 9, 2010. htpp://www. kurdishmedia.com (accessed August 25, 2010).

———. "The Rise of a New Ottoman Empire: The Trap of Interfaith Dialogue." *Kurdish Aspects.* 2008. http://kurdishaspects.com (accessed July 5, 2010).

National Post. *McMaster's atomic PR fight.* April 21, 2007. http://www.canada.com/nationalpost/news/story.html?id=84126f69-db8a-441d-ae94-f2c7dcec05b9&p=1 (accessed October 13, 2010).

New Message. 2000a. www.yenimesaj.com.tr. September 23, 2000

New Message. 2000b. www.yenimesaj.com.tr. May 6, 2000

New Message. 2000c. www.yenimesaj.com.tr. June 7,8,, 2000

New Message. 2000d. www.yenimesaj.com.tr. June 17, 2000

Kamermeerderheid Eist Onderzoek Naar Turkse Beweging. Directed by Erik-Jan Zürcher. Performed by NOVA. 2008.

Özdalga, Elisabeth. 2005. "Redeemer or Outsider? The Gülen Community in the Civilizing Process." *Muslim World* 95, 3:429-446.

Özkök, Ertuğrul. 1995. "Röportaj." *Hürriyet*, January 23.

Perincek, Dogu. "ABD'nin NATO Ulkelerini Kontrol Orgutu: SuperNATO." *Aydinlik*, November 2, 2007.

———. "ORG. EŞREF BİTLİS'İ KATLETTİREN GLADYO TAYYİP ERDOĞAN'I İKTİDARA GETİRDİ." *Aydinlik*, October 21, 1996.

Pipes, Daniel. "'Rushdie Rules' reach Florida." *The Washington Times*, September 20, 2010.

Poyraz, Ergun. *Amerika'daki İmam.* Togan Yayincilik, 2009.

———. *Fethullah'in Gercek Yuzu.* Otopsi Yayinlari, 2000.

———. *Kanla Abdest Alanlar.* Togan Yayincilik, 2007.

———. *Musa'nin AKP'si.* Togan Yayincilik, 2007.

———. *Musa'nin AKP'si.* Togan Yayincilik, 2007.

———. *Musa'nın Çocukları Tayyip ve Emine.* Togan Yayincilik, 2007.

———. *Musa'nin Cocuklari, Tayyip ve Emine.* Togan Yayincilik, 2007.

———. *Musa'nın Gülü.* Togan Yayincilik, 2007.

———. *Musa'nın Gülü.* Togan Yayincilik, 2007.

———. *Musa'nın Mücahiti.* Togan Yayincilik, 2007.

————. *Said-i Nursi'den Demirel ve Ecevit'e Fethullah'ın Gerçek Yüzü.* Otopsi Yayinlari, 2000.

Rodgers, Guy. "Fethulla Gulen: Infiltrating the U.S. Through Our Charter Schools?." *Act for America.* 2010. htpp://actforamerica.org (accessed June 5, 2010).

Rubin, Michael. 2008. Turkey's Turning Point Could there be an Islamic Revolution in Turkey? National Review Online. Retrieved May 2, 2009 Rubin, Michael. «Fethullah Gulen Speaks.» *National Review Online*, 2010. (http://article.nationalreview.com/?q=NWZlOGJmZDQ2NGYwMmIwZWYxYTYx ZTAwZTIxYzl3ZGY=)

Ryan, Thomas. 2007. "The Gulen Movement." National Catholic Reporter, August 17.

Savas, Vural. "Ugur Mumcu'nun Olum Fermani Olan Yazi." *Aydinlik Magazine,* January 28, 2007: 64.

Saribay, Ali Y. 1995. "Differences Should Not Lead to Separation" *Milliyet*, August 10.

Saritoprak, Zeki. 2001. "Fethullah Gülen: A Sufi in His Own way." Paper delivered at the conference Islamic Modernities: Fethullah Gülen and Contemporary Islam, Georgetown University, 26-27 April, Washington, DC.

Saritoprak, Zeki and Sidney Griffith. 2005. "Fethullah Gülen and the 'People of the Book': A Voice from Turkey for Interfaith Dialogue." *Muslim World* 95, No 3:329-340.

Saritoprak, Zeki. 2005. "Introduction." *Muslim World* 95, No 3: 262-271.

Schevitz, Tanya. "Professors want own names put on Mideast blacklist." *San Francisco Chronicle* , September 28, 2002.

Schwartz, Stephen. "Islamist Gülen Movement Runs U.S. Charter Schools." *Islamist Watch.* March 29, 2010. htpp://islamist-watch.org (accessed July 12, 2010).

Senoglu, Ruhsar, and Serdar Bolat. "Fethullah'in Fetvasi Uygulandi, Hz. Muhammed'I Kelime-I Sehadet'ten Cikardilar!" *Aydinlik*, November 2, 2007.

Sezgin, Ismet. "SİYONİZMİN İSLAMCI MÜRİTLERİ." *Milli Cozum*, May 1, 2007.

————. "Zaman'cilar Ehli Kitap midir?" *Milli Cozum*, September 1, 2005.

Sharon-Krespin, Rachel. "Fethullah Gülen's Grand Ambition." *Middle East Quarterly*, 2009: Volume 16 Issue 1 pp55-66.

Statement of the president Suleyman Demirel. 1999. *Anatolia,* June 19.

Statement of the Prime Minister Bulent Ecevit. 1999. *Anatolia,* June 22.

Stenhouse, Paul. "Islam's trojan horse? Turkish nationalism and the Nakshibendi Sufi order". Quadrant Magazine; Dec, Vol. 51 Issue 12, p11-18

Taraf. *Ergenekon'da gözaltı ve dava.* Istanbul retrived from http://www.taraf.com.tr/ haber/20030.htm, October 27, 2008.

Tavernise, Sabrina. "Turkish Schools Offer Pakistan a Gen$er Vision of Islam." *The New York Times*, May 4, 2008.

Tedik, Fatih M. 2007. " Gulen Movement as an Integration Mechanism for the Europe's Turkish and Muslim Community: Potentials and Constraints." Pp. 230-245 in the conference proceeding Muslim World in Transition: Contributions of Gulen Movement. London, England: Leeds University Press.

Tempo, "Fethullah Hoca." 1997 *Tempo*, February 7, pp. 46-50.

Today's Zaman. "Ergenekon File." *Today's Zaman*, 2009.

Tuncer, Faruk. 2006. "Foundations of the Intellectual Development of Fethullah Gülen." Paper presented at the conferenceon Islam in the Contemporary World: The Fethullah Gülen Movement in Thought and Practice, Southern Methodist University, March 3-4, Dallas, Texas.

Turk Okullari. 1996. *Hurriyet*, November 3.

Türker, Abdulhamid. "Hypocrisy in languages: criticizing Fethullah Gülen, English or Turkish? ." *Today's Zaman*, November 19, 2009.

Fethullahçı Gladyo Belgeseli . Performed by Ulusal TV. 2009.

Unal, Ali and Alphonse Williams. 2000. *Advocate of Dialogue*, Fairfax, Virginia: The Fountain.

Veren, Nurettin. *Kuşatma / ABD'nin Truva Atı Fethullah Gülen Harekatı .* Istanbul: Siyah Beyaz Yayin, 2007.

Webb, Lynn. "Die-Hard Enemies of Fethullah Gulen." *Fethullah Gulen.* January 24, 2003. http://www.fethullahgulen.org/press-room/239-fethullah-gulen-is-there-more-to-him-than-meets-the-eye/1215-die-hard-enemies-of-fethullah-gulen.html (accessed September 3, 2010).

Willaims, Ian. 2005. "An Absent Influence? The Nurcu/Fetullah Gülen Movements in Turkish Islam and their potential influence upon European Islam and global education." Paper presented at the conference on Islam in the Contemporary World: The Fethullah Gülen Movement in Thought and Practice, Rice University, November 12-13, Houston, Texas.

Williams, Paul. ""Exclusive: Has the Universal Caliphate Emerged from Pennsylvania? Is the CIA Serving the Needs of an Islamist? (Part Two)" ." *thelastcrusade.org.* 2010. http://www.thelastcrusade.org (accessed August 12, 2010).

———. "Exclusive: Obama Administration turns Blind Eye to Muslim Foreign Militia in Pennsylvania." *Family Security Matters.* April 9, 2010. htpp://www .familysecuritymatters.org (accessed July 19, 2010).

———. "Fethullah Gulen: Working for the Islamic Caliphate from Saylorsburg, PA." *sheikyermami.* April 6, 2010. http://www.sheikyermami.com (accessed July 8, 2010).

———. "PENNSYLVANIA PERFECT STAGING AREA FOR NEXT 9/11." *The Last Crusade.* May 7, 2010. htpp://www.thelastcrusade.com (accessed August 22, 2010).

———. *The Last Crusade.* March 3, 2010. http://thelastcrusade.org/category/the-last -crusade/ (accessed September 2, 2010).

———. *The Last Crusade.* 2010. www.thelastcrusade.org (accessed August 12, 2010).

———. *The Last Crusade.* March 25, 2010. http://thelastcrusade.org/?s=obama (accessed September 9, 2010).

Woodhall, Ruth. "Organizing the Organization, Educating the Educators: An Examination of Fethullan Gülen's Teaching and the Membership of the Movement."." *Proceedings from Islam in the Contemporary World: The Fethullah Gülen Movement in Thought and Practice.* Rice University, Houston, 2005.

World Bank. *Gross Domestic Product:Data for 2007.* World Bank, 2008 (accessed May 12, 2009).

Yanardag, Merdan. *Bir ABD Projesi Olarak AKP.* Istanbul: Siyah Beyaz Yayın, 2007.

———. *Bir ABD Projesi Olarak AKP.* Siyah Beyaz Yayin, 2007.

———. *Türkiye Nasıl Kuşatıldı? / Fethullah Gülen Hareketinin Perde Arkası* . Siyah Beyaz Yayinlari, 2006.

———. *Türkiye Nasıl Kuşatıldı? / Fethullah Gülen Hareketinin Perde Arkası.* Siyah Beyaz Yayin, 2006.

Yavuz, Hakan. 2004. "The Gülen Movement: a modern expression of Turkish Islam - Interview with Hakan Yavuz." *Religioscope,* July 21.

Yavuz, Hakan and John Espesito. 2003. *Turkish Islam and the Secular State: The Gülen Movement.* New York: Syracuse University Press.

Yilan, Orhan. "TÜRKİYE'Yİ HIRİSTİYANLAŞTIRMAK VEYA İSLAMİYETİ ILIMLAŞTIRMAK." *Milli Cozum,* November 6, 2006.

Zaman, Amberin. "How far they have travelled ." *The Economist,* March 6, 2008.

Zelyut, Riza. "Nedir bu ADL?" *Gunes,* August 27, 2007.

Appendix

Dataset

	Author	Title	Date	Publisher	Language	Gülen	Type
1	Ergun Poyraz	Musa'nın Çocukları Tayyip ve Emine	2007	Togan Yayıncılık	Turkish	1	book
2	Ergun Poyraz	Musa'nın Gülü	2007	Togan Yayıncılık	Turkish	1	book
3	Ergun Poyraz	Musa'nın Mücahiti	2007	Togan Yayıncılık	Turkish	1	book
4	Ergun Poyraz	Patlak Ampul	2007	Togan Yayıncılık	Turkish	1	book
5	Ergun Poyraz	Musa'nin AKP'si	2007	Gökbörü Yayıncılık	Turkish	1	book
6	Ergun Poyraz	Kanla Abdest Alanlar	2007	Togan Yayıncılık	Turkish	1	book
7	Ergun Poyraz	Amerika'daki İmam	2009	Togan Yayıncılık	Turkish	1	book
8	Ergun Poyraz	Misyonerler Arasında Altı Ay Dünden Bugüne Hıristiyanlığın Ve Yahudiliğin Analizi	2004	Toplumsal Dönüşüm Yayınları	Turkish	1	book
9	Ergun Poyraz	Tarikat, Siyaset, Ticaret ve Cinayet Masonlarla El Ele	2009	Togan Yayıncılık	Turkish	1	book
10	Ergun Poyraz	Said-i Nursi'den Demirel ve Ecevit'e Fethullah'ın Gerçek Yüzü	2000	Otopsi Yayınları	Turkish	1	book
11	Ergun Poyraz	Fethullah'in Gercek Yuzu	2000	Otopsi Yayınları	Turkish	1	book

	Author	Title	Date	Publisher	Language	Gülen	Type
12	Merdan Yanardag	Türkiye Nasıl Kuşatıldı? / Fethullah Gülen Hareketinin Perde Arkası	2006	Siyah Beyaz Yayın	Turkish	1	book
13	Merdan Yanardag	Bir ABD Projesi Olarak AKP	2007	Siyah Beyaz Yayın	Turkish	1	book
14	Hikmet Cetinkaya	Fethullah Gülen'in 40 Yıllık Serüveni	2004	Günizi Yayıncılık	Turkish	1	book
15	Hikmet Cetinkaya	Fethullah Gülen'in 40 Yıllık Serüveni 2. Kitap	2005	Günizi Yayıncılık	Turkish	1	book
16	Hikmet Cetinkaya	Fethullah Gülen ABD ve AKP	2007	Günizi Yayıncılık	Turkish	1	book
17	Hikmet Cetinkaya	Din Baronunun Kazları	2006	Günizi Yayıncılık	Turkish	1	book
18	Hikmet Cetinkaya	Fethullahçı Gladyo	2008	Günizi Yayıncılık	Turkish	1	book
19	Hikmet Cetinkaya	Amerikan Mızıkacıları	2009	Cumhuriyet Kitaplari	Turkish	1	book
20	Hikmet Cetinkaya	Soros'un Çocukları	2008	Cumhuriyet Kitaplari	Turkish	1	book

	Author	Title	Date	Publisher	Language	Gülen	Type
21	Hikmet Cetinkaya	Yobaz ve Hokkabaz	2008	Cumhuriyet Kitapları	Turkish	1	book
22	Hikmet Cetinkaya	Kuzu Postunda Kurt Tarikat Siyaset Ticaret	2007	Günizi Yayıncılık	Turkish	1	book
23	Hikmet Cetinkaya	Türkiye'nin Şeytan Üçgeni / Tarikat - Siyaset - Ticaret	2007	Günizi Yayıncılık	Turkish	1	book
24	Soner Yalcin	Bu Dinciler O Müslümanlara Benzemiyor	2009	Doğan Kitap	Turkish	1	book
25	Nurettin Veren	Kuşatma / ABD'nin Truva Atı Fethullah Gülen Harekatı	2007	Siyah Beyaz Yayın	Turkish	1	book
26	Aytunç Erkin	Fethullah Hoca'nın Şifreleri	2005	Kaynak Yayinlari	Turkish	1	book
27	Semih Tufan Gülaltay	Fethullah Müslüman Mı?	2006	İleri Yayınları	Turkish	1	book
28	Alpaslan Işıklı	SAID NURSİ,FETHULLAH GÜLEN VE "LAİK" SEMPATİZANLARI	1998	Hasat Yayinlari	Turkish	1	book
29	Necip Hablemitoglu	Kostebek	2003	Toplumsal Dönüşüm Yayınları	Turkish	1	book

	Author	Title	Date	Publisher	Language	Gülen	Type
30	Necip Hablemitoglu	Kostebek	2003	Toplumsal Dönüşüm Yayınları	Turkish	2	book
31	Hulki Cevizoğlu	Nurculuk Dünü Bugünü Said Nursiden Müslüm Gündüz Ve Fethullah Gülen'e	1999	Beyaz Yayınları	Turkish	2	book
32	Faik Bulut	Kim bu Fethullah Gülen	1999	Ozan Yayincilik	Turkish	2	book
33	Faik Bulut	Hoca'nin Okullari	1998	STKB	Turkish	2	book
34	Emin Koc	Belgelerle Dinlerarası Diyalog Misyonerleri	n.d		Turkish	1	book
35	M. Emin Değer	Bir Cumhuriyet Düşmanının Portesi ya da Fethullah Gülen Hocaefendinin derin misyonu	2000	Cumhuriyet Kitaplari	Turkish	1	book
36	M. Emin Değer	Bir Cumhuriyet Düşmanının Portesi ya da Fethullah Gülen Hocaefendinin derin misyonu	2000	Cumhuriyet Kitaplari	Turkish	2	book
37	Vural Savaş	İrtica ve Bölücülüğe Karşı Militan Demokrasi	2000	Bilgi Yayinevi	Turkish	2	book
38	Vural Savaş	Dip Dalgası	2006	Bilgi Yayinevi	Turkish	1	book

	Author	Title	Date	Publisher	Language	Gülen	Type
39	Vural Savaş	Emperyalizmin Uşakları İhanetin Belgeleri	2008	Bilgi Yayinevi	Turkish	1	book
40	Vural Savaş	Türkiye Cumhuriyeti Çökerken	2008	Bilgi Yayinevi	Turkish	1	book
41	Vural Savaş	Vatanın Bağrına Düşman Dayamış Hançerini	2007	Bilgi Yayinevi	Turkish	1	book
42	Zübeyir Kındıra	Fethullahın Copları	2001	Su yayınları	Turkish	2	book
43	Kaan Turhan	Ergenekon ve Fethullah Yeni Osmanlı Misyonu'yla Kürdistan İnşası	2010	Asya Safak Yayinlari	Turkish	1	book
44	Aytunç Altındal	Vatikan ve Tapınak Şövalyeleri	2004	Alfa Yayinlari	Turkish	1	book
45	Rachel Sharon-Krespin	Fethullah Gülen's Grand Ambition: Turkey's Islamist Danger	2/2/2009	Middle East Forum	English	2	Journal
46	Michael Rubin	Turkey's Turning Point	14/4/2008	National Review Online	English	2	Journal
47	Paul Stenhouse	Islam's trojan horse? Turkish nationalism and the Nakshibendi Sufi order	12/1/2007	Quadrant	English	2	Journal

	Author	Title	Date	Publisher	Language	Gülen	Type
48	Mehmet Sevket Papa ile Gizli Anlasma Eygi		5/26/2000	Milli Gorus	Turkish	1	News Paper
49	Mehmet Sevket Turk Dunyasi Eygi		5/5/2000	Milli Gazate	Turkish	1	News Paper
50	Aland Mizell	The Rise of a New Ottoman Empire: The Trap of Interfaith Dialogue	10/1/2007	Kurdishaspect.com	English	2	website
51	Aland Mizell	Erdogan's AKP, Fethullah Gülen's opium, and the Kurdish Question	4/15/2005	Kurdish Media	English	2	website
52	jane's report	Turkey's third power	2/1/2009	Jane's Islamic Affairs Analyst	English	2	Report
53	Soner Cagaptay	What's Really Behind Turkey's Coup Arrests?	2/25/2010	Foreign Policy	English	2	Magazine
54	Soner Cagaptay	Behind Turkey's Witch Hunt	5/16/2009	Newsweek	English	2	Magazine
55	Michael Rubin	Fethullah Gülen Speaks	4/6/2010	National Review Online	English	2	Journal
56	Paul Williams	FETHULLAH Gülen: THE PENNSYLVANIA PASHA FINALLY EXPOSED	3/14/2010	thelastcrusade.org	English	2	weblog

	Author	Title	Date	Publisher	Language	Gülen	Type
57	Michelle Fowler	West Texas Charter School May Have Ties to Radical Islam	6/1/2010	cbs7kosa.com	English	2	webnews
58	Paul Williams	Gülen MOVEMENT PAVES WAY FOR NEW ISLAMIC WORLD ORDER BILLIONS POUR INTO Gülen'S COF-FERS FROM DRUG TRADE	7/21/2010	thelastcrusade.org	English	2	weblog
59	Paul Williams	Gülen MOVEMENT PAVES WAY FOR NEW ISLAMIC WORLD ORDER BILLIONS POUR INTO Gülen'S COF-FERS FROM DRUG TRADE	7/21/2010	thelastcrusade.org	English	1	weblog
60	Paul Williams	Gülen MOVEMENT GENER-ATES WINDS OF WORLD WAR	6/2/2010	babbazeesbrain. blogspot.com	English	2	weblog
61	Debbie	Enough is Enough	6/4/2010	Right Truth	English	2	weblog
62	Paul Williams	ISRAEL FACES SHOWDOWN	6/2/2010	thelastcrusade.org	English	2	weblog
63	masonlar. azeriblog.com	FETULLAH GülenIN MAS-KASI CIRILDI	6/6/2010	masonlar.azeriblog.com	Turkish	1	weblog

	Author	Title	Date	Publisher	Language	Gülen	Type
64	David Goldman	Fethullah Gülen's cave of wonders	6/9/2010	Asia Times	English	2	webnews
65	Myke	America TAXPAYERS ALLOWED TO 'WRITE OFF' DONATIONS TO TERRORIST SCHOOLING!	6/12/2010	desertconservative.com	English	2	weblog
66	Paul Williams	Exclusive: White House Muslim Advisor Supports Islamist Gülen Movement	6/15/2010	familysecuritymatters.com	English	2	weblog
67	Guy Rodgers	Fethullah Gülen: Infiltrating the U.S. Through Charter Schools	6/16/2010	This Generation	English	2	weblog
68	Michael Rubin	Wilson Center's Award to Davutoglu	6/17/2010	the corner	English	2	weblog
69	Paul Williams	ISLAM RULES THE WEST TEXAS TAQIYYA	6/21/2010	babbazeesbrain.blogspot.com	English	2	weblog
70	Paul Williams	Gülen Movement Engulfs Lone Star State	6/22/2010	familysecuritymatters.com	English	2	weblog
71	J Murrah	Tag Archive for 'Gülen-movement'	6/22/2010	texaslos.com	English	2	weblog

	Author	Title	Date	Publisher	Language	Gülen	Type
72	Right Side News	Islamist Gülen Movement Runs U.S. Charter Schools	6/25/2010	socialismisnottheanswer.com	English	2	weblog
73	Paul Williams	Gülen MOVEMENT FUNDED BY HEROIN VIA THE C.I.A.	6/28/2010	thelastcrusade.org	English	2	weblog
74	BGuzzardi	Kenny Gamble aka Luqman Abdul Haqq; Fethullah Gülen; CAIR & Taqiyya	7/7/2010	The Conservative Reform Network Blog	English	2	weblog
75	rick murphy	Fethullah Gülen is Rebelling Aganist the Democratic Republic of Turkiye	7/4/2010	google groups	English	2	webgroup
76	Mizgîn	GÜLEN, THE CIA, AND THE AMERICAN DEEP STATE	6/28/2008	rastibini.blogspot.com	English	1	weblog
77	Mizgîn	IN SIBEL'S CROSSHAIRS: FETHULLAH GÜLEN, CENTRAL ASIA, AND BEYOND	7/11/2008	rastibini.blogspot.com	English	1	weblog
78	Paul Williams	WORLD WAR III ARISES FROM ANKARA (AND PENNSYLVANIA)	6/5/2010	thelastcrusade.org	English	2	weblog
79	Devvy Kidd	We must stop the drive for Sharia Law in America	7/26/2010	devvy.com	English	2	weblog

	Author	Title	Date	Publisher	Language	Gülen	Type
80	Aland Mizell	Does terrorism help Gülen's Muslim missionaries? A first class revolution from the bottom up	9/8/2010	kurdishmedia.com	English	2	weblog
81	Paul Williams	Backlash for Fethullah Gülen's Jihad: U.S. Court Upholds Reality Of Armenian Genocide	14/8/2010	familysecuritymatters.com	English	2	weblog
82	Thomas Benson	Gülen Watch	n.d	Gülenwatch.blogspot.org	English	2	weblog
83	Hugh Fitzgerald	Fitzgerald: Ayatollah Khomeini and Fethullah Gülen	7/4/2010	jihadwatch.com	English	2	weblog
84	Paul Williams	IS WALMART FUNDING RADICAL ISLAMIC SCHOOLS IN USA?	22/8/2010	thelastcrusade.org	English	2	weblog
85	Babbazee	This Ain't Yer Ma's Walton Family	23/8/2010	babbazeesbrain.blogspot.com	English	2	weblog
86	Babbazee	Who TF is Fethullah Gülen and Why Should You Care?	7/4/2010	babbazeesbrain.blogspot.com	English	2	weblog
87	Babbazee	Super Caliph Fatalish And Worse Than Halitosis	27/4/2010	babbazeesbrain.blogspot.com	English	2	weblog

	Author	Title	Date	Publisher	Language	Gülen	Type
88	Babbazee	Stupid Caliphs Fatefully Invade You By Osmosis!	28/4/2010	babbazeesbrain.blogspot.com	English	2	weblog
89	Paul Williams	CIA SERVES "WORLD'S MOST DANGEROUS ISLAMIST"	27/4/2010	thelastcrusade.org	English	2	weblog
90	Babbazee	Covert PA Caliphate Infects Us With Necrosis	8/5/2010	babbazeesbrain.blogspot.com	English	2	weblog
91	Paul Williams	PA: PERFECT STAGING AREA FOR NEXT 9/11	7/5/2010	thelastcrusade.org	English	2	weblog
92	Babbazee	Gülen's CIA Smack Cash	28/6/2010	babbazeesbrain.blogspot.com	English	2	weblog
93	Babbazee	Fuller Shit!	20/7/2010	babbazeesbrain.blogspot.com	English	2	weblog
94	noname	Who has been called "the most dangerous Islamist on earth," Gülen , a Turkish Preacher.	23/8/2010	actforamericaomaha.com	English	2	website
95	noname	Is Walmart Wealth Funding Radical Islamic Schools in the U.S.A.?	24/8/2010	thetwomalcontents.com	English	2	website

	Author	Title	Date	Publisher	Language	Gülen	Type
96	Paul Williams	Exclusive: Education Jihad Sweeps the Country – A Guide to the Gülen Schools in America	22/4/2010	familysecuritymatters.com	English	2	website
97	Guy Rodgers	Fethullah Gülen: Infiltrating the U.S. Through Our Charter Schools?	n.d	actforamerica.org	English	2	website
98	Babbazee	Stupid Rich Confabulater Funding Mo's Necrosis	24/5/2010	babbazeesbrain.blogspot.com	English	2	weblog
99	Paul Williams	CIA AND U.S. STATE DEPARTMENT FUND NEW ISLAMIC WORLD ORDER	27/4/2010	thelastcrusade.org	English	2	weblog
100	Paul Williams	CIA AND U.S. STATE DEPARTMENT FUND NEW ISLAMIC WORLD ORDER	27/4/2010	thelastcrusade.org	English	1	weblog
101	Paul Williams	World's 'Most Dangerous Islamist' Alive, Well, and Living in Pennsylvania	n.d	familysecuritymatters.com	English	2	weblog
102	Sheikyermami	Fethullah Gülen: Working for the Islamic Caliphate from Saylorsburg, PA	6/4/2010	windsofjihad.com	English	2	weblog

	Author	Title	Date	Publisher	Language	Gülen	Type
103	Roberto Santiago	Muslim Militias in America against America is a-OK!	9/4/2010	thechroniclewatch.com	English	2	weblog
104	noname	Fethullah Gülen is a "CIA Illegal Operations"	16/5/2010	stichingturkeli.blogspot.org	English	2	weblog
105	noname	Fethullah Gülen is a "CIA Illegal Operations"	16/5/2010	stichingturkeli.blogspot.org	English	1	weblog
106	noname	Fetullah Gülen, America's Khomeini	7/4/2010	theiconoclast.com	English	2	website
107	Stephen Schwartz	Islamist Gülen Movement Runs U.S. Charter Schools	29/3/2010	freedomwatch.com	English	2	website
108	BGuzzardi	Fethullah Gülen in the Poconos	19/5/2010	thelastcrusade.org	English	2	website
109	BabbaZee	ISLAMIC ARMED FORTRESS EMERGES FROM POCONO MOUNTAINS	6/4/2010	thelastcrusade.org	English	2	website
110	Tel-Chai Nation	Islamic Gülen movement running US charter schools	17/4/2010	doubletriangle.com	English	2	website
111	Paul Williams	ISLAMIC SOLDIERS INVADE SAYLORSBURG PA.	9/4/2010	thelastcrusade.org	English	2	website

	Author	Title	Date	Publisher	Language	Gülen	Type
112	Stephen Schwartz	Islamist Gülen Movement Runs U.S. Charter Schools	29/3/2010	Islamist-watch.org	English	2	website
113	Stephen Schwartz	Islamist Gülen Movement Runs U.S. Charter Schools	29/3/2010	Europenews.dk	English	2	website
114	Hugh Fitzgerald	Khomeini and Fethullah Gülen: Same Evil, Different Beard	n.d	thelastcrusade.org	English	2	website
115	Guy Rodgers	Fethullah Gülen: Infiltrating the U.S. Through Our Charter Schools? [incl. Tarek ibn Ziyad Academy]	8/4/2010	actmidwestnews. blogspot.com	English	2	weblog
116	Wayne Madsen	Mossad implicated in a coup plot in Turkey, a NATO country; CIA fingerprints also found on attempt	4/12/2008	onlinejournal.com	English	1	website
117	Wayne Madsen	Mossad implicated in a coup plot in Turkey, a NATO country; CIA fingerprints also found on attempt	4/12/2008	onlinejournal.com	English	2	website
118	Mizgin	NEWS THAT'S NOT FIT TO PRINT IN AMERICA	10/9/2006	rastibini.blogspot.com	English	1	weblog

	Author	Title	Date	Publisher	Language	Gülen	Type
119	Mizgin	NEWS THAT'S NOT FIT TO PRINT IN AMERICA	10/9/2006	rastibini.blogspot.com	English	2	weblog
120	Paul Williams	Exclusive: Obama Administration turns Blind Eye to Muslim Foreign Militia in Pennsylvania	9/4/2010	familysecuritymatters.com	English	2	website
121	Teomankaiser	Paul Williams: Gülen & CIA	5/12/2010	teomankaiser.blogspot.com	English	2	weblog
122	midnight rider	POCONO MOUNTAINS: NEW HAVEN FOR TERRORISTS?	7/5/2010	ibloga.blogspot.com	English	2	weblog
123	Aland Mizell	Gülen and academic research: Propaganda tour to Turkey and for the Gülen Movement	17/3/2010	KurdishMedia.com	English	2	website
124	Don Morris	Radical Islamic Schools Thrive Throughout America	21/4/2010	docstalk.blogspot.com	English	2	weblog
125	Robert Spencer	Symposium: The World's Most Wanted: A "Moderate Islam"	15/6/2010	frontpagemag.com	English	2	website
126	Burhan Gurdogan	The Gülen Movement is a danger spreading from Turkey to the world	30/1/2010	thecommentfactory.com	English	2	website

	Author	Title	Date	Publisher	Language	Gülen	Type
127	Burhan Gurdogan	The Gülen Movement : Cult influence over the Justice and Development Party (AKP)	10/5/2010	thelastcrusade.org	English	2	website
128	noname	Turkification, Islamization is alive and well in the USA	13/5/2010	rightruth.typepad.com	English	2	weblog
129	David Livingstone	Uighur Nationalism, Turkey and the CIA	31/7/2009	eldib.wordpress.com	English	2	weblog
130	Paul Williams	UNIVERSAL CALIPH- ATE EMERGES FROM PENNSYLVANIA	28/4/2010	thelastcrusade.org	English	2	weblog
131	Roy Schestowitz	Where Gates Wealth Goes	31/5/2010	techrights.org	English	2	website
132	noname	Why the Turkish ship started the fight in Gaza? The flotilla is the perfect cover up	31/5/2010	koolnews.wordpress. com	English	2	weblog
133	Don Morris	World's 'Most Dangerous Is- lamist' Alive, Well, and Living in Pennsylvania	7/4/2010	docstalk.blogspot.com	English	2	weblog
134	Acik Istihbarat	Fethullah Sebekesinin Baglantilari	n.d	acikistihbarat.com	Turkish	1	website

	Author	Title	Date	Publisher	Language	Gülen	Type
135	noname	FETHULLAH GÜLEN-SİYONİZM İLİŞKİSİ ve İŞBİRLİĞİ	n.d	hanifiislam.com.tr	Turkish	1	website
136	noname	FETHULLAH GÜLEN'İN İLİŞKİ ve İŞBİRLİĞİNDE BULUNDUGU SİYONİSTLER: Richard Perle, Morton Abramowitz, ADL(Anti-Defamation League)		hanifiislam.com.tr	Turkish	1	website
137	Ergun Poyraz	Fethullah'ın Gerçek Yüzü	n.d	hanifiislam.com.tr	Turkish	1	website
138	Rıza Zelyut	Nedir bu ADL	8/27/2007	Gunes	Turkish	1	News Paper
139	Rıza Zelyut	Fethullahçı Müslümanlar uyanın	10/1/2007	Gunes	Turkish	1	News Paper
140	Milli Çözüm Araştırma Ekibi	FETULLAH GÜLEN DOSYASI	12/1/2004	Milli Cozum	Turkish	1	Magazine
141	Milli Çözüm Araştırma Ekibi	AKP'nin PERDE ARKASI	12/1/2004	Milli Cozum	Turkish	1	Magazine

	Author	Title	Date	Publisher	Language	Gülen	Type
142	Ahmet Akgul	FİTNETULLAH VE BAYKAL	5/18/2010	Milli Cozum	Turkish	1	Magazine
143	Osman Eraydin	Fetullahçılar ve Barzanilerle İyi İlişkiler Kurabilen DİYARBAKIR VALİLERİ, ÜST GÖREVLERE ATANIYORDU!	7/22/2010	Milli Cozum	Turkish	1	Magazine
144	Nail Kizilkan	AKP KURMAYLARININ "BASIN ÖZGÜRLÜĞÜ" ANLAYIŞI VE "ACI SON"UN YAKLAŞMASI	6/24/2010	Milli Cozum	Turkish	1	Magazine
145	Ismet Sezgin	ÖLÇÜ ERDOĞAN VE FETULLAH MI, YOKSA KUR'AN VE RESULÜLLAH MI?	6/21/2010	Milli Cozum	Turkish	1	Magazine
146	Ahmet Akgul	İSRAİL SALDIRISINA KARŞI;İSLAM DÜŞMANLARININ, DİN İSTİSMARCILARININ VE AKP YANDAŞLARININ ORTAK TELAŞI!	6/8/2010	Milli Cozum	Turkish	1	Magazine

Appendix

	Author	Title	Date	Publisher	Language	Gülen	Type
147	Ramazan Yucel	DANIŞTAY SALDIRISININ OYAK VE FETULLAH CEMAATİ BAĞLANTILARI	5/24/2010	Milli Cozum	Turkish	1	Magazine
148	Nejat Hakkul	MİLLİ GAZETE'NİN FET-ULLAHÇI YAZARLARI VE YANILGILARI	5/24/2010	Milli Cozum	Turkish	1	Magazine
149	Orhangazi Yilmayan	FETULLAHÇILARIN RÜYASI MI, YOKSA ŞİFRELİ CIA UYARISI MI?	4/29/2010	Milli Cozum	Turkish	1	Magazine
150	Osman Eraydin	TSK'YA SATAŞILMASI VE KANCIKLARIN ŞAPŞALLAŞMASI!	2/23/2010	Milli Cozum	Turkish	1	Magazine
151	Yakup Gozubuyuk	"Ergenekon"da İlginç İddialar İçeren Bir Dilekçe SİYONİST SENARYOLAR SORGULANIYORDU!	11/23/2009	Milli Cozum	Turkish	1	Magazine
152	Yakup Gozubuyuk	KÜRTLEŞMİŞ YAHUDİLERLE İSRAİL İLİŞKİLERİ, PKK-FETULLAH-CILIK İŞBİRLİĞİ	10/28/2009	Milli Cozum	Turkish	1	Magazine

	Author	Title	Date	Publisher	Language	Gülen	Type
153	Bayram Yonem	FETULLAHCILIK, KÜRE-SEL EMPERYALİZMİN BİR ARACIDIR	9/19/2009	Milli Cozum	Turkish	1	Magazine
154	Ahmet Akgul	KÜRT AÇILIMI VE HIYANET ALÇAKLIĞI	8/21/2009	Milli Cozum	Turkish	1	Magazine
155	Zeynep Basyazar	BAŞBUĞ'UN ABD ZİYARETİ VE RAHATSIZ ETTİKLERİ	7/25/2009	Milli Cozum	Turkish	1	Magazine
156	Osman Eraydin	SİYONİST NETANYAHU "OR-DUSUZ FİLİSTİN" İSTİYOR... Bizdeki Sabataist Cunta ise;ORDUYU ZAYIFLAT-MAYA ÇALIŞIYOR!	7/25/2009	Milli Cozum	Turkish	1	Magazine
157	Ramazan Yucel	FETULLAHÇILARIN TELAŞI!?	6/25/2009	Milli Cozum	Turkish	1	Magazine
158	Osman Eraydin	FETULLAHÇILARLA BARZANİ İTTİFAKI VE F. TİPİ YAPILANMANIN İFLASI	6/25/2009	Milli Cozum	Turkish	1	Magazine
159	Bayram Yonem	GAVURLARA "NÜKLEER GÜCÜ," MÜSLÜMANLARA "HOŞGÖRÜYÜ" REVA GÖRENLER	6/25/2009	Milli Cozum	Turkish	1	Magazine

	Author	Title	Date	Publisher	Language	Gülen	Type
160	Bayram Yonem	GKB İLKER BAŞBUĞ'UN SÖZLERİ VE TÜRKÇESİ	5/23/2009	Milli Cozum	Turkish	1	Magazine
161	Bayram Yonem	İnsanları Allah İle Aldatan, Ama Şeytan Amerika'ya Çalışan: BİR FİGÜRAN; FETHULLAH GÜLEN	4/27/2009	Milli Cozum	Turkish	1	Magazine
162	Nevzat Gunduz	ENCÜMENİ DANİŞ VE EMEKLİ GENERALLER	3/25/2009	Milli Cozum	Turkish	1	Magazine
163	Ufuk Efe	SÜLEYMAN KARAGÜLLE'NİN MİLLİ ÇÖZÜM İLE İLGİLİ SAP-TAMALARI, YAŞAR NURİ ÖZTÜRK'ÜN SAPTIRMALARI	3/25/2009	Milli Cozum	Turkish	1	Magazine
164	Ahmet Akgul	TSK'YI KISITLAMA VE KISTIRMA HAZIRLIKLARI	3/25/2009	Milli Cozum	Turkish	1	Magazine
165	Nevzat Gunduz	MİT ESKİSİ MAHİR'İN ÇAR-PITMA VE İFTİRA ATMA MAHARETİ	3/4/2009	Milli Cozum	Turkish	1	Magazine
166	Ahmet Akgul	ERGENEKON'UN AÇILIMI: IRKÇI EMPERYALİZM AT DEĞİŞTİRİYOR!	3/4/2009	Milli Cozum	Turkish	1	Magazine

	Author	Title	Date	Publisher	Language	Gülen	Type
167	Bayram Yonem	İSRAİL UŞAKLIĞI VE TSK DÜŞMANLIĞI	1/29/2009	Milli Cozum	Turkish	1	Magazine
168	Mehmet Deniz	ERGENEKON MASALI VE TUNCAY GÜNEY MAVALI	12/29/2008	Milli Cozum	Turkish	1	Magazine
169	Nail Kizilkan	ABD'NİN RECEP ERDOĞAN'I VE BARAK OBAMA'NIN YULARI	12/29/2008	Milli Cozum	Turkish	1	Magazine
170	Nail Kizilkan	RECEP ERDOĞAN OF THE USA AND THE REINS OF BARACK OBAMA	12/29/2008	Milli Cozum	English	1	Magazine
171	Hakan Ekmekci	ÖCALAN CUMHURBAŞKANI, FETULLAH DİYANET VE DİYALOG BAKANI!	11/24/2008	Milli Cozum	Turkish	1	Magazine
172	Ufuk Efe	YARGININ YAMULMASI VE HAKİMEVİ SKANDALI	10/24/2008	Milli Cozum	Turkish	1	Magazine
173	Milli Çözüm Araştırma Ekibi	VAR MISINIZ, MASON LO-CALARINA MAHKEME AÇMAYA?!	8/23/2008	Milli Cozum	Turkish	1	Magazine

	Author	Title	Date	Publisher	Language	Gülen	Type
174	Ahmet Akgul	"Orduya Hücum!" Operasyonu:BİR ERGENEKOMİK SE-NARYOSU VE CIA-FETUL-LAHÇI FİYASKOSU	8/8/2008	Milli Cozum	Turkish	1	Magazine
175	Necati Akgul	PENTAGON-ERGENEKON HATTI	7/28/2008	Milli Cozum	Turkish	1	Magazine
176	Orhan Yilan	BAYRAM DEĞİL, SEYRAN DEĞİL, KRALİÇE BİZİ, NIYE ÖPMEK İSTEMİŞTİ?	6/26/2008	Milli Cozum	Turkish	1	Magazine
177	Orhan Yilan	WHAT WAS THE REASON FOR THE UNEXPECTED VISIT OF QUEEN?	6/26/2008	Milli Cozum	Turkish	1	Magazine
178	Bayram Yonem	PENTAGON ERGENEKON HATTI	6/4/2008	Milli Cozum	Turkish	1	Magazine
179	Ufuk Efe	"MİLLİ"CİLİK Mİ, "ULUSAL"CILIK MI?	6/4/2008	Milli Cozum	Turkish	1	Magazine
180	Nevzat Gunduz	AKP'Yİ KAPATMA DAVASI VE MASONİK CEPHENİN TELAŞI	4/30/2008	Milli Cozum	Turkish	1	Magazine

	Author	Title	Date	Publisher	Language	Gülen	Type
181	Bayram Yonem	Bu Yırtık, Dikiş Tutmayacak!... ÖNCE BULANACAK, SONRA DURULACAK MI?	4/30/2008	Milli Cozum	Turkish	1	Magazine
182	Ufuk Efe	AYIN AYNASI	2/2/2004	Milli Cozum	Turkish	1	Magazine
183	Orhangazi Yilmayan	"YAHUDA"YI TANIMAYAN VE İSLAM'A DAYANMA-YAN HERKES SİYONİZMİN HİZMETKÂRIDIR!	7/22/2010	Milli Cozum	Turkish	1	Magazine
184	Abdullah Akgul	"MARDİN FETVASINDAN" SONRA, RIFAT BÖREKÇİNİN ANKARA FETVASINI DA GEREKSİZ VE GEÇERSİZ SAYACAKLAR MIYDI?	7/22/2010	Milli Cozum	Turkish	1	Magazine
185	Ufuk Efe	KEMALİZMİN MUCİDİ; MOİZ KOHEN (M.TEKİNALP) YAHUDİSİ	7/22/2010	Milli Cozum	Turkish	1	Magazine
186	Mikail Yilmaz	OLAYLARA GLOBAL BAKIŞ	6/24/2010	Milli Cozum	Turkish	1	Magazine
187	Aykut Ozubuyuk	ODA TV'NİN, ODALIK TEPKİSİ	6/24/2010	Milli Cozum	Turkish	1	Magazine

Author	Title	Date	Publisher	Language	Gülen	Type
188 Zeynep Basyazar	SİYONİST GÜDÜMLÜ BATININ PANZEHİRİ VE ERBAKAN'IN SİLAH TEKNOLOJİLERİ	6/24/2010	Milli Cozum	Turkish	1	Magazine
189 Ahmet Akgul	İSRAİL SALDIRI-SINA KARŞI:İSLAM DÜŞMANLARININ, DİN İSTİSMARCILARININ VE AKP YANDAŞLARININ OR-TAK TELAŞI!	6/8/2010	Milli Cozum	Turkish	1	Magazine
190 Nevzat Gunduz	İSRAİL'İN MANYAKLIĞI, AKP'NİN MÜNAFIKLIĞI	5/31/2010	Milli Cozum	Turkish	1	Magazine
191 Milli Çözüm Araştırma Ekibi	ERHAN GÖKSEL'İN SIR ÖLÜMÜYLE, DENİZ BAYKAL KOMPLOSUNUN BAĞLANTILARI	5/25/2010	Milli Cozum	Turkish	1	Magazine
192 Abdullah Akgul	MÜNAFIKLAR ARAMIZDA MI, YOKSA TARİHİN MEZARLIĞINDA MI?	5/24/2010	Milli Cozum	Turkish	1	Magazine

	Author	Title	Date	Publisher	Language	Gülen	Type
193	Ufuk Efe	TÜRKİYE'DE DERİN DEVLET SAVAŞLARI VE MUHTEMEL SONUÇLARI	5/24/2010	Milli Cozum	Turkish	1	Magazine
194	Ahmet Akgul	ABD'NİN ZIRVA ZİRVESİ VE AKP'NİN İRAN TERTİBİ	5/24/2010	Milli Cozum	Turkish	1	Magazine
195	Mikail Yilmaz	CEMAATLER, GENERALLER VE İHTİMALLER	4/29/2010	Milli Cozum	Turkish	1	Magazine
196	Ahmet Akgul	SICAK YAZ YAKLAŞIYOR VE İRAN KUŞATILIYOR!	4/16/2010	Milli Cozum	Turkish	1	Magazine
197	Ismet Sezgin	DÜNYA EN BÜYÜK DÖNÜŞÜME HAZIRLANIYOR;MASONLUK VE SİYONİZM CAN ÇEKİŞİYOR!	3/24/2010	Milli Cozum	Turkish	1	Magazine
198	Ahmet Akgul	BAŞBUĞ'UN BAŞAĞRISI VE MİLLİ VİCDANIN: "YETER!" ÇAĞRISI	3/24/2010	Milli Cozum	Turkish	1	Magazine
199	Ramazan Yucel	SİYASALLAŞAN YARGININ YARALANMASI VE İSTİSMARCI DİN YARASALARI	2/23/2010	Milli Cozum	Turkish	1	Magazine

	Author	Title	Date	Publisher	Language	Gülen	Type
200	Ismet Sezgin	ABD'NİN KÜRTLERİ VE Demokratik Açılım İsteyen TEKSASLILARIN AKIBETİ!	2/23/2010	Milli Cozum	Turkish	1	Magazine
201	Nail Kizilkan	31 MART VAK'ASINDAN ER-GENEKON DALGASINA	1/24/2010	Milli Cozum	English	1	Magazine
202	Yakup Gozubuyuk	Ey Asker ve Sivil, Bütün Millet! YA ERBAKAN'IN ADİL DÜZENİNE RAZI OLACAKSINIZ, VEYA AMERİKA'NIN ZİLLETİNE KATLANACAKSINIZ!	1/24/2010	Milli Cozum	Turkish	1	Magazine
203	Osman Eraydin	RECEP TAYYİP EKİBİNİN DÖNEKLEŞİP DEĞERLENMESİ!	1/24/2010	Milli Cozum	English	1	Magazine
204	Nevzat Gunduz	DERSİM DERSLERİ VE İKİYÜZLÜLÜK TERESLERİ	12/21/2009	Milli Cozum	Turkish	1	Magazine
205	Mikail Yilmaz	AKP'NİN VURGUN ŞEBEKESİ VE MAFYA EKONOMİSİ	11/23/2009	Milli Cozum	Turkish	1	Magazine
206	Osman Eraydin	AÇILIM EDEBİYATI VEYA HIYANETİN YOL HARİTASI	11/23/2009	Milli Cozum	Turkish	1	Magazine

	Author	Title	Date	Publisher	Language	Gülen	Type
207	Nejat Hakkul	"FİTNE" KAVRAMI VE Bediüzzaman'a göre "UMUMİ SELAMET" İNKILÂBI	10/28/2009	Milli Cozum	Turkish	1	Magazine
208	Ramazan Yucel	İSLAM LİBERALİZMİ SAF- SATASI VE HOŞGÖRÜ SALATASI	9/19/2009	Milli Cozum	Turkish	1	Magazine
209	Osman Eraydin	SOYGUN DÜZENİ, SİYASET VE MEDYA	9/19/2009	Milli Cozum	Turkish	1	Magazine
210	Yakup Gozubuyuk	ALÇAKLIĞIN BELGESİ VE "NAMUZSUZ"LARIN AKIBETİ	9/19/2009	Milli Cozum	Turkish	1	Magazine
211	Abdullah Akgul	PKK'YA SAYGI, TSK'YA SALDIRI	9/19/2009	Milli Cozum	Turkish	1	Magazine
212	Ahmet Akgul	İRAN'I VURMAK İÇİN, İSRAİL YOLA ÇIKTI	9/19/2009	Milli Cozum	Turkish	1	Magazine
213	Milli Çözüm Araştırma Ekibi	YÖNETİCİLERİMİZİ KİM YÖNETİYOR?	2/2/2004	Milli Cozum	Turkish	1	Magazine

	Author	Title	Date	Publisher	Language	Gülen	Type
214	Osman Eraydin	ABD'NİN ARSIZ POLİTİKASI VE AKP'NİN AYARSIZ PALAVRASI	2/2/2004	Milli Cozum	Turkish	1	Magazine
215	Milli Çözüm Araştırma Ekibi	DİNİ VE MİLLİ HAREKETLERDEKİ KRİPTO (GİZLİ) YAHUDİLER	10/2/2004	Milli Cozum	Turkish	1	Magazine
216	Selman Yucel	SİYONİZM'İN SÖMÜRÜ SALTANATI VE ABD'NİN BORÇLANDIRMA BARBARLIĞI	10/2/2004	Milli Cozum	Turkish	1	Magazine
217	Halil Yaman	TAYYİB BEY'İN TABİATI: Her Sözünden Geri Adım Attı!	11/2/2004	Milli Cozum	Turkish	1	Magazine
218	Ufuk Efe	ERBAKAN'I YABAN AN-LADI, ŞABAN ANLAMADI	10/1/2006	Milli Cozum	Turkish	1	Magazine
219	Mehmet Deniz	İRTİCA MEVCUTTUR VE EN SİNSİ SORUNDUR!	11/6/2006	Milli Cozum	Turkish	1	Magazine
220	Nevzat Gunduz	TÜRKİYE YOL AYRIMINDA	11/6/2006	Milli Cozum	Turkish	1	Magazine

	Author	Title	Date	Publisher	Language	Gülen	Type
221	Orhan Yilan	TÜRKİYE'Yİ HIRİSTİYANLAŞTIRMAK VEYA İSLAMİYETİ ILIMLAŞTIRMAK	11/6/2006	Milli Cozum	Turkish	1	Magazine
222	Osman Eraydin	ADNAN OKTAR, OLTAYA MI TAKILDI?	11/6/2006	Milli Cozum	Turkish	1	Magazine
223	Erdogan Piskin	BİR ÇETE ARANIYOR	9/1/2006	Milli Cozum	Turkish	1	Magazine
224	Orhan Yilan	FETTULLAHCILARIN "FETTANL"LIĞI	9/1/2006	Milli Cozum	Turkish	1	Magazine
225	Tevfik Bala	ILIMLI İSLAM TUZAĞI	9/1/2006	Milli Cozum	Turkish	1	Magazine
226	Mikail Yilmaz	FEHMİ KORU: BİLDERBERG "VAAZ" CISI MI YAPILDI?	8/1/2006	Milli Cozum	Turkish	1	Magazine
227	Orhan Yilan	FETULLAH GÜLEN'İN KURTULUŞ YOLU!	8/1/2006	Milli Cozum	Turkish	1	Magazine
228	Osman Eraydin	HÜKÜMETİN HABERİ VAR MIYDI?	7/1/2006	Milli Cozum	Turkish	1	Magazine
229	Ufuk Efe	CIA'NIN HİLAFET HAZIRLIĞI ve "VAİZ" PAZARLIĞI	7/1/2006	Milli Cozum	Turkish	1	Magazine

	Author	Title	Date	Publisher	Language	Gülen	Type
230	Necati Akgul	AMERİKA GÖÇÜYOR VE FETULLAHÇILAR FİRAVUNA GÜVENİYOR!	7/1/2006	Milli Cozum	Turkish	1	Magazine
231	Abdullah Akgul	BEDİÜZZAMAN'A İFTİRA	6/1/2006	Milli Cozum	Turkish	1	Magazine
232	Nevzat Gunduz	SİNSİ BİR PROJENİN PERDE GERİSİ VE DİN ADINA MASUM BİR HİZMETİN HIYANETE DÖNÜŞMESİ	5/1/2006	Milli Cozum	Turkish	1	Magazine
233	Nail Kizilkan	BAĞNAZLIĞIN FATURASI VE FİKRET OTYAM'IN TUTARSIZLIĞI	3/1/2006	Milli Cozum	Turkish	1	Magazine
234	Ismet Sezgin	FİRAVUNLAR VE FİGÜRANLAR	3/1/2006	Milli Cozum	Turkish	1	Magazine
235	Okan Ekinci	GARİP AMA GERÇEK!	3/1/2006	Milli Cozum	Turkish	1	Magazine
236	Ufuk Efe	VURAL SAVAŞ'IN TARİHİ TESPİTLERİ VE FETULLAH TEHLİKESİ	2/1/2006	Milli Cozum	Turkish	1	Magazine

	Author	Title	Date	Publisher	Language	Gülen	Type
237	Abdullah Akgul	SÜLEYMAN KARAGÜLLE'NİN KÖR GÜLLELERİ	2/1/2006	Milli Cozum	Turkish	1	Magazine
238	Mikail Yilmaz	HİLAL HAÇLI SAVAŞI VE ILIMLI İSLAMCILARIN SAFI	2/1/2006	Milli Cozum	Turkish	1	Magazine
239	Nail Kizilkan	TARİH BOYUNCA DİN İSTİSMARI	2/1/2006	Milli Cozum	Turkish	1	Magazine
240	Mikail Yilmaz	ŞU DÖRT TARİHİ UNUTMAYALIM!..	1/1/2006	Milli Cozum	Turkish	1	Magazine
241	noname	ARSLANOĞLU KÖYLÜLERİ: ESARETTEN CUMHURİYETE	12/1/2005	Milli Cozum	Turkish	1	Magazine
242	Osman Eraydin	TÜRKİYE, SURİYE VE İRAN'I SATTI MI? AKP, ABD nin Truva Atı mı?	12/1/2005	Milli Cozum	Turkish	1	Magazine
243	Nevzat Gunduz	YAŞAR BÜYÜKANIT PAŞA MI HAKLI, YOKSA; ÖMER LÜTFİ METE MAŞA MI?	11/1/2005	Milli Cozum	Turkish	1	Magazine
244	Mehmet Deniz	BİR DOĞRUYU, YANLIŞ AMAÇLAR İÇİN KULLANMAK	9/1/2005	Milli Cozum	Turkish	1	Magazine

	Author	Title	Date	Publisher	Language	Gülen	Type
245	Ismet Sezgin	"ZAMAN"CILAR EHLİ KİTAP MI DIR?	9/1/2005	Milli Cozum	Turkish	1	Magazine
246	Ufuk Efe	SEFERBERLİK SORUŞTURMASI YA, AKP VE F. GÜLEN ALEYHİNE SONUÇLANIRSA!?	2/1/2010	Milli Cozum	Turkish	1	Magazine
247	Nevzat Gunduz	ERBAKAN'I ÖNLEMEK İÇİN, DİĞER İSLAMCI HAREKETLERİN DESTEKLENMESİ	8/1/2005	Milli Cozum	Turkish	1	Magazine
248	Tevfik Bala	MİLLİ DUYARSIZLIK VE TUTARSIZLIK	6/1/2005	Milli Cozum	Turkish	1	Magazine
249	Halil Yaman	MÜBAHALE - LANETLEŞME	6/1/2005	Milli Cozum	Turkish	1	Magazine
250	Osman Eraydin	LAİKLİK, MİSYONERLİK VE ATATÜRK	1/1/2005	Milli Cozum	Turkish	1	Magazine
251	Ismet Sezgin	AYIN AYNASI	6/1/2005	Milli Cozum	Turkish	1	Magazine
252	Ahmet Akgul	PUTİN'İN HAYIRLI YAKLAŞIMI VE ARMEGE-DON SAVAŞI	1/1/2005	Milli Cozum	Turkish	1	Magazine

	Author	Title	Date	Publisher	Language	Gülen	Type
253	Ismet Sezgin	FETULLAHÇILARIN MARAZI VE KUR'ANIN MESAJI	1/1/2007	Milli Cozum	Turkish	1	Magazine
254	Necati Akgul	EKÜMENLİK FECAETİ VE DİYANET'İN DENAETİ	1/1/2007	Milli Cozum	Turkish	1	Magazine
255	Kazim Gulfidan	YENİ OLUŞUMUN ESKİ OYUNCAKLARI!	1/1/2007	Milli Cozum	Turkish	1	Magazine
256	Hakan Ekmekci	YENİ OSMANLICILIK, NATO'NUN YENİÇERİSİ OLMAKTIR!...	2/1/2007	Milli Cozum	Turkish	1	Magazine
257	Orhan Yilan	"İBRAHİM YOLU" MU, "ABRAHAM OYUNU" MU?	2/1/2007	Milli Cozum	Turkish	1	Magazine
258	Tevfik Bala	AKP, UÇURUMA YAKLAŞAN ABD DOLMUŞUNA MUAVİNLİK YAPIYOR!	2/1/2007	Milli Cozum	Turkish	1	Magazine
259	Oguzhan Cildir	"AYDINLIK"IN AYIBI VE AKP'NİN ARSIZLIĞI	3/1/2007	Milli Cozum	Turkish	1	Magazine
260	Kazim Gulfidan	FETULLAH GÜLEN'İN KEHANETİ VE HİRANT DİNK CİNAYETİ	3/1/2007	Milli Cozum	Turkish	1	Magazine

	Author	Title	Date	Publisher	Language	Gülen	Type
261	Mehmet Deniz	DERİN HESAPLAŞMA VE MİLLİ JANDARMA	3/1/2007	Milli Cozum	Turkish	1	Magazine
262	Oguzhan Cildir	KARMAŞIK İLİŞKİLER VE ÇELİŞKİLER	3/1/2007	Milli Cozum	Turkish	1	Magazine
263	Necmeddin Biskin	MASONLUK VE DİNLERARASI DİYALOG İLİŞKİSİ VE SIYONİSTLERİN ERBAKAN ENDİŞESİ	4/1/2007	Milli Cozum	Turkish	1	Magazine
264	Nail Kizilkan	MASON TARİKATÇILARI VE ATATÜRKÇÜLÜK SAHTEKÂRLARI	5/1/2007	Milli Cozum	Turkish	1	Magazine
265	Ismet Sezgin	SİYONİZMİN İSLAMCI MÜRİTLERİ	5/1/2007	Milli Cozum	Turkish	1	Magazine
266	Oguzhan Cildir	FETULLAH MI, FİTNETULLAH MI?	5/1/2007	Milli Cozum	Turkish	1	Magazine
267	Ahmet Akgul	AKP AMİGOLARINI, AMERİKA BİLE KURTARA-MADI VE CHP ÇILKINI ÇIKARDI	5/1/2007	Milli Cozum	Turkish	1	Magazine

	Author	Title	Date	Publisher	Language	Gülen	Type
268	Nevzat Gunduz	FETULLAHÇILAR, CAMİLERİ KİLİSE GİBİ, KÜLTÜR EVİ YAPACAK MI?	6/1/2007	Milli Cozum	Turkish	1	Magazine
269	Nevzat Gunduz	FETULLAH GÜLEN ŞEBEKESİ, SİYONİST ABD'NİN MİSYONERLERİ Mİ?	7/1/2007	Milli Cozum	Turkish	1	Magazine
270	Nail Kizilkan	SAFINI BİLMEYEN YA SAFTIR VEYA SAHTEKÂRDIR!	8/1/2007	Milli Cozum	Turkish	1	Magazine
271	Oguzhan Cildir	SEVENLERİNİN DİLİNDEN FETHULLAH GÜLEN	8/1/2007	Milli Cozum	Turkish	1	Magazine
272	Ahmet Akgul	DERİN AMERİKA'NIN GÜNDEMİ NİYE TÜRKİYE?	8/1/2007	Milli Cozum	Turkish	1	Magazine
273	Orhan Yilan	Bilderberg ve CFR Tarihinde Bir İlk : BU İKİ SİYONİST KURULUŞ AYNI TARİHLERDE NİYE TÜRKİYE DE	9/1/2007	Milli Cozum	Turkish	1	Magazine

	Author	Title	Date	Publisher	Language	Gülen	Type
274	Bayram Yonem	Yahudi Samanıyla Beslenen Zamancılara Cevap:AKP NİN LÜBNAN HIYANETİ VE BÖLGEMİZİN FELAKETİ	9/1/2007	Milli Cozum	Turkish	1	Magazine
275	Ahmet Deniz	DOSTU AMERİKA OLANIN POSTU MEZATA ÇIKAR!	9/1/2007	Milli Cozum	Turkish	1	Magazine
276	Tevfik Bala	F.GÜLEN VE S. DEMİREL TÜRKİYE'Yİ AKP'LEŞTİRİYOR,İSRAİL AKP'Yİ İSLAMSIZLAŞTIRIYOR	10/1/2007	Milli Cozum	Turkish	1	Magazine
277	Oguzhan Cildir	VİCDANLI HIRİSTİYAN,MÜNAFIK MÜS-LÜMANDAN HAYIRLIDIR!	10/1/2007	Milli Cozum	Turkish	1	Magazine
278	Osman Eraydin	SİYONİST SERMAYENİN 'NGO'LARI VE EMPERYALİZMİN SİVİL LEJYONLARI	11/1/2007	Milli Cozum	Turkish	1	Magazine
279	Emin Koc	GÜLEN, RTE VE AVANESİ ADL HIZMETÇISI	5/10/2005	Yeni Mesaj	Turkish	1	News Paper

	Author	Title	Date	Publisher	Language	Gülen	Type
280	Emin Koc	YAHUDİ MAFYASI ADL ve GÜLEN İLİŞKİSİ	4/6/2005	Yeni Mesaj	Turkish	1	News Paper
281	Emin Koc	Zaman mı saptırıyor Ahmet Şahin mi?	6/18/2001	Yeni Mesaj	Turkish	1	News Paper
282	Emin Koc	AB ve misyonerlik	10/18/2003	Yeni Mesaj	Turkish	1	News Paper
283	Emin Koc	Diyalogcuların "küresel bela"sı	4/28/2004	Yeni Mesaj	Turkish	1	News Paper
284	Emin Koc	Misyonerliğin dik âlası	5/15/2004	Yeni Mesaj	Turkish	1	News Paper
285	Emin Koc	"İbrahimî dinler kavramı"nın patenti kadim müşriklere ait	5/18/2004	Yeni Mesaj	Turkish	1	News Paper
286	Emin Koc	Zaman'dan Gülerce'ye niçin acıyorum?	12/27/2004	Yeni Mesaj	Turkish	1	News Paper
287	Emin Koc	Müslümanları, papazların kucağına nasıl sürüklüyorlar?	12/29/2004	Yeni Mesaj	Turkish	1	News Paper
288	Emin Koc	Bak şu "Nurcu Papaz"ın yaptığına!	12/31/2004	Yeni Mesaj	Turkish	1	News Paper

	Author	Title	Date	Publisher	Language	Gülen	Type
289	Emin Koc	"Müslüman kılıklı rahipler"i tanımak için "foyametre"	1/19/2005	Yeni Mesaj	Turkish	1	News Paper
290	Emin Koc	Rahiplerin örümcek ağları	1/26/2005	Yeni Mesaj	Turkish	1	News Paper
291	Emin Koc	Hayrettin Karaman ne diyor bu işlere?	2/22/2005	Yeni Mesaj	Turkish	1	News Paper
292	Emin Koc	ABD'de Yahudi mafyası: ADL ve Gülen Efendi'nin diyalog masalı	3/23/2005	Yeni Mesaj	Turkish	1	News Paper
293	Emin Koc	Papazlarınızı ve hahamlarınızı da yanlarınıza alarak geliniz!	4/1/2005	Yeni Mesaj	Turkish	1	News Paper
294	Emin Koc	Al sana bir nurcu papaz daha ey pişkin diyalogcu!	4/2/2005	Yeni Mesaj	Turkish	1	News Paper
295	Emin Koc	Al sana "ABD'de Yahudi mafyası: ADL" ve "Gülen Efendi'nin ADL teklifli diyalog masalı"	4/6/2005	Yeni Mesaj	Turkish	1	News Paper
296	Emin Koc	Bunlar kimin çocukları?	4/7/2005	Yeni Mesaj	Turkish	1	News Paper

	Author	Title	Date	Publisher	Language	Gülen	Type
297	Emin Koc	Hz. Muhammed sevgisini oltanın ucuna takmak	4/13/2005	Yeni Mesaj	Turkish	1	News Paper
298	Emin Koc	ADL'de kesiştiren hikmet ne?	6/11/2005	Yeni Mesaj	Turkish	1	News Paper
299	Emin Koc	Dinlerarası diyalog bir Vatikan kurumu	7/7/2005	Yeni Mesaj	Turkish	1	News Paper
300	Emin Koc	Uzaktan kumandalı dinlerarası diyalogun stratejik boyutu	7/14/2005	Yeni Mesaj	Turkish	1	News Paper
301	Emin Koc	Diyalog'ta çok yüzlülük esası	7/19/2005	Yeni Mesaj	Turkish	1	News Paper
302	Emin Koc	Diyalogcuların terörizm istismarı	7/26/2005	Yeni Mesaj	Turkish	1	News Paper
303	Emin Koc	"Diyalogcu kel"lerin barış ilacı	7/27/2005	Yeni Mesaj	Turkish	1	News Paper
304	Emin Koc	Diyalogcuların işbu yeni rivayet Mesihiyet anlayışı	7/28/2005	Yeni Mesaj	Turkish	1	News Paper
305	Emin Koc	Şimdi de katolik nikahlı "medeniyetler ittifaki"	7/29/2005	Yeni Mesaj	Turkish	1	News Paper

	Author	Title	Date	Publisher	Language	Gülen	Type
306	Emin Koc	Elhamdülillah, Ahmed Şahin bir adım attı, şimdi sıra Zaman'da…	8/18/2005	Yeni Mesaj	Turkish	1	News Paper
307	Emin Koc	Bayram üstü sahnelenen diyalog zenneliği	12/15/2005	Yeni Mesaj	Turkish	1	News Paper
308	Emin Koc	ABD'nin koynundaki diyalogcu nurcular ve üstatları	12/17/2005	Yeni Mesaj	Turkish	1	News Paper
309	Emin Koc	"Hristiyan nur talebeleri"	12/21/2005	Yeni Mesaj	Turkish	1	News Paper
310	Emin Koc	ADL, İslam'a ve Türklüğe hizmet ediyormuş da haberimiz yokmuş…	12/26/2005	Yeni Mesaj	Turkish	1	News Paper
311	Emin Koc	Papazın ölüsünden medet umanlar	2/10/2006	Yeni Mesaj	Turkish	1	News Paper
312	Emin Koc	"Diyalogcu olmama hakkı" yok!	2/11/2006	Yeni Mesaj	Turkish	1	News Paper
313	Emin Koc	Diyalogcuların karikatürü	2/24/2006	Yeni Mesaj	Turkish	1	News Paper
314	Emin Koc	Kur'an-ı Kerim'in "İncilleştirilmesi" ve "İncil'li mealci"nin itirafları	3/11/2006	Yeni Mesaj	Turkish	1	News Paper

	Author	Title	Date	Publisher	Language	Gülen	Type
315	Emin Koc	Diyalogcu nurcunun "İncilli meali"nden BOP'un "Furkan'ül Hakk"ına	3/14/2006	Yeni Mesaj	Turkish	1	News Paper
316	Emin Koc	"İncilli meal" üreten bozacı ve diyalogcu şahidi şiracı	3/15/2006	Yeni Mesaj	Turkish	1	News Paper
317	Emin Koc	Rasulüllah'ın ikazından "İncilli meal üretenler"in payına düşen	3/16/2006	Yeni Mesaj	Turkish	1	News Paper
318	Emin Koc	Bir değil bin tane Karaman olsa ne yazar	3/17/2006	Yeni Mesaj	Turkish	1	News Paper
319	Emin Koc	"Sultan Hamid'in emriyle tımarhaneye kadar sürüklendim"	4/21/2006	Yeni Mesaj	Turkish	1	News Paper
320	Emin Koc	ABD'nin "yeşil kuşağı" ekseninde Said Nursî–İnönü ittifakı	4/22/2006	Yeni Mesaj	Turkish	1	News Paper
321	Emin Koc	BOP işgalleri öncesi toplum mühendisliği	4/24/2006	Yeni Mesaj	Turkish	1	News Paper
322	Emin Koc	Papaz eli öpenler, neden cami duvarını kirletmeye kalkışıyorlar?	5/25/2006	Yeni Mesaj	Turkish	1	News Paper
323	Emin Koc	Papanın küfürleri ve Türkiyeli papağanları	9/16/2006	Yeni Mesaj	Turkish	1	News Paper

	Author		Title	Date	Publisher	Language	Gülen	Type
324	Emin Koc	'Diyalogcu nurcu'lar kendilerine yeni Papa arıyorlar		9/19/2006	Yeni Mesaj	Turkish	1	News Paper
325	Emin Koc	AKP'den "Fetullahçı yerine Nakşibendi versek" manevrası		10/9/2006	Yeni Mesaj	Turkish	1	News Paper
326	Emin Koc	MHP'deki "F tipi" değişim...		11/24/2006	Yeni Mesaj	Turkish	1	News Paper
327	Emin Koc	Papa'larını "güya inkâra kalkışan"lar		11/25/2006	Yeni Mesaj	Turkish	1	News Paper
328	Emin Koc	Mandacılar ve ortak özellikleri		12/3/2006	Yeni Mesaj	Turkish	1	News Paper
329	Emin Koc	Cinayetlerin "F tipi" ipuçları ve AKP'nin dut yemiş bülbülleri		2/14/2007	Yeni Mesaj	Turkish	1	News Paper
330	Emin Koc	Hem papazlık, hem imamlık bir arada yapılır mı?		3/30/2007	Yeni Mesaj	Turkish	1	News Paper
331	Emin Koc	Diyaloğun çocuklarının cinay-etleri bunlar		4/27/2007	Yeni Mesaj	Turkish	1	News Paper
332	Emin Koc	Takke-tespih maskeli Haçlı ittifakçılarının foyası		4/15/2009	Yeni Mesaj	Turkish	1	News Paper

	Author	Title	Date	Publisher	Language	Gülen	Type
333	Emin Koc	ETÖ ile F-ETÖ	5/1/2009	Yeni Mesaj	Turkish	1	News Paper
334	Emin Koc	Saçları ağarmış Zeybek'e acırım	12/10/2009	Yeni Mesaj	Turkish	1	News Paper
335	Aziz Karaca	"Türkiye'de ılımlı İslam iktidardadır"	5/21/2004	Yeni Mesaj	Turkish	1	News Paper
336	Aziz Karaca	Ulemanın 'diyalog'tan anladıkları	5/22/2004	Yeni Mesaj	Turkish	1	News Paper
337	Aziz Karaca	Papalık Konseyi misyonunun parçasından verir misiniz?	5/26/2004	Yeni Mesaj	Turkish	1	News Paper
338	Aziz Karaca	"Hizmet" hezimete döndü duydun mu?	1/20/2005	Yeni Mesaj	Turkish	1	News Paper
339	Aziz Karaca	Gülen'le röportaj furyası	1/28/2005	Yeni Mesaj	Turkish	1	News Paper
340	Aziz Karaca	Diyaloga karşıyız, çünkü…	2/18/2005	Yeni Mesaj	Turkish	1	News Paper
341	Aziz Karaca	Diyalog çarpmış yamyassı olmuş	3/1/2005	Yeni Mesaj	Turkish	1	News Paper

	Author	Title	Date	Publisher	Language	Gülen	Type
342	Aziz Karaca	Diyalog çarpmış yamyassı olmuş-2	3/2/2005	Yeni Mesaj	Turkish	1	News Paper
343	Aziz Karaca	Vatikan tarafından sulanan diyalog meyveleri	5/20/2005	Yeni Mesaj	Turkish	1	News Paper
344	Aziz Karaca	Kovayı uzatan Müslümansa, Hoşgörü muslukları kuruyor	6/1/2005	Yeni Mesaj	Turkish	1	News Paper
345	Aziz Karaca	"Erzurum Kongresi'nden Abant Platformuna" öyle mi?	6/19/2005	Yeni Mesaj	Turkish	1	News Paper
346	Aziz Karaca	Bu vakfın sicili tartışmalı	6/20/2005	Yeni Mesaj	Turkish	1	News Paper
347	Aziz Karaca	Abant Platformu için Erzurum yanlış bir seçim	6/22/2005	Yeni Mesaj	Turkish	1	News Paper
348	Aziz Karaca	Nene Hatun'un torunlarına soruyoruz	6/23/2005	Yeni Mesaj	Turkish	1	News Paper
349	Aziz Karaca	Perşembenin gelişi Çarşambadan bellidir	6/24/2005	Yeni Mesaj	Turkish	1	News Paper
350	Aziz Karaca	İşte o vakfın bir kitabı ve seyreyleyin gümbürtüyü	6/26/2005	Yeni Mesaj	Turkish	1	News Paper

	Author	Title	Date	Publisher	Language	Gülen	Type
351	Aziz Karaca	Camileri konser salonu yapmak!	6/29/2005	Yeni Mesaj	Turkish	1	News Paper
352	Aziz Karaca	Yaktığınız mumlarla memleket alev alev	6/30/2005	Yeni Mesaj	Turkish	1	News Paper
353	Aziz Karaca	Sam amcanın nefesiyle dönen değirmenler	7/1/2005	Yeni Mesaj	Turkish	1	News Paper
354	Aziz Karaca	Hıristiyanlığın ılımlısı çıkmadı mı daha?	9/2/2005	Yeni Mesaj	Turkish	1	News Paper
355	Aziz Karaca	Zaman'ın bir teklifi var	9/17/2005	Yeni Mesaj	Turkish	1	News Paper
356	Aziz Karaca	"Hizmet" hezimete döndü duydun mu?	9/20/2005	Yeni Mesaj	Turkish	1	News Paper
357	Aziz Karaca	Papazların şahsında katillere kucak açmak	10/8/2005	Yeni Mesaj	Turkish	1	News Paper
358	Aziz Karaca	Bir konu iki kalem mandacılar bir alem	10/10/2005	Yeni Mesaj	Turkish	1	News Paper
359	Aziz Karaca	Diyalog coğrafyamıza döşenen bir mayındır	10/28/2005	Yeni Mesaj	Turkish	1	News Paper

	Author	Title	Date	Publisher	Language	Gülen	Type
360	Aziz Karaca	Diyalogcuların dikkatine!...	11/9/2005	Yeni Mesaj	Turkish	1	News Paper
361	Aziz Karaca	Haçlılardan himmet görenleri görmüyor musun?	11/14/2005	Yeni Mesaj	Turkish	1	News Paper
362	Aziz Karaca	Bu yolu açanlara lanet olsun	1/1/2006	Yeni Mesaj	Turkish	1	News Paper
363	Aziz Karaca	Hocaefendi Vatikan'a bir daha gitse iyi olur!	4/20/2006	Yeni Mesaj	Turkish	1	News Paper
364	Aziz Karaca	Başına 'diyalog' tuğlası düşmüş adamlar	5/11/2006	Yeni Mesaj	Turkish	1	News Paper
365	Aziz Karaca	Beşer şaşar, Faruk Beşer de şaşar	6/22/2006	Yeni Mesaj	Turkish	1	News Paper
366	Aziz Karaca	Diyalogcuların ipliği bir kez daha pazarda	7/30/2006	Yeni Mesaj	Turkish	1	News Paper
367	Aziz Karaca	BOP'un boynuzu kulağı görünmüşken...	8/16/2006	Yeni Mesaj	Turkish	1	News Paper
368	Aziz Karaca	ABD'ye 'hayır,' ABD'cilere 'evet' olur mu?	8/18/2006	Yeni Mesaj	Turkish	1	News Paper

	Author	Title	Date	Publisher	Language	Gülen	Type
369	Aziz Karaca	'Papa Cenapları ve Saz Arkadaşları'	8/20/2006	Yeni Mesaj	Turkish	1	News Paper
370	Aziz Karaca	Sahibinin sesi	8/30/2006	Yeni Mesaj	Turkish	1	News Paper
371	Aziz Karaca	Zaman okuyorsanız...	9/20/2006	Yeni Mesaj	Turkish	1	News Paper
372	Aziz Karaca	Diyalog ikliminde ihanete şeref diyorlar	10/28/2006	Yeni Mesaj	Turkish	1	News Paper
373	Aziz Karaca	Zaman neye tekabül eder?	11/29/2006	Yeni Mesaj	Turkish	1	News Paper
374	Aziz Karaca	"Diyalogun bir adım sonrası işgaldir"	12/22/2006	Yeni Mesaj	Turkish	1	News Paper
375	Aziz Karaca	Diyalogcu medya büyüyormuş!	1/10/2007	Yeni Mesaj	Turkish	1	News Paper
376	Aziz Karaca	Büyüyen ve büyütülen nedir?	1/12/2007	Yeni Mesaj	Turkish	1	News Paper
377	Aziz Karaca	Zaman her zamanki gibi...	2/1/2007	Yeni Mesaj	Turkish	1	News Paper

	Author	Title	Date	Publisher	Language	Gülen	Type
378	Aziz Karaca	Hacım şehit cenazesinde, ce-binde Zaman	3/18/2007	Yeni Mesaj	Turkish	1	News Paper
379	Aziz Karaca	İftar haberlerini harmanlarsak…	9/23/2007	Yeni Mesaj	Turkish	1	News Paper
380	Aziz Karaca	'Ya başka bir Kur'an getir ya da onu değiştir'	10/4/2007	Yeni Mesaj	Turkish	1	News Paper
381	Aziz Karaca	Bizi öğüten değirmenlere su taşıyan yine biz	10/28/2007	Yeni Mesaj	Turkish	1	News Paper
382	Aziz Karaca	Gülen hareketi: Mazlumlara sızlanmak yasak	11/1/2007	Yeni Mesaj	Turkish	1	News Paper
383	Aziz Karaca	"Batı asla düşmanımız değil"miş!	11/2/2007	Yeni Mesaj	Turkish	1	News Paper
384	Aziz Karaca	Tecdit mi tahrip mi?	11/6/2007	Yeni Mesaj	Turkish	1	News Paper
385	Aziz Karaca	Kaleyi kazmalayan birileri var	11/8/2007	Yeni Mesaj	Turkish	1	News Paper
386	Aziz Karaca	Çırpındıkça batmak bu olsa gerek	11/9/2007	Yeni Mesaj	Turkish	1	News Paper

	Author	Title	Date	Publisher	Language	Gülen	Type
387	Aziz Karaca	Bir sualim var	11/26/2007	Yeni Mesaj	Turkish	1	News Paper
388	Aziz Karaca	Uyan!	12/11/2007	Yeni Mesaj	Turkish	1	News Paper
389	Aziz Karaca	Lord Ahmet'in renkli misafirleri	12/18/2007	Yeni Mesaj	Turkish	1	News Paper
390	Aziz Karaca	Kime ve neye hizmet?	1/15/2008	Yeni Mesaj	Turkish	1	News Paper
391	Aziz Karaca	Misyoner minare çalar, Diya- logcu kılıf hazırlar	1/16/2008	Yeni Mesaj	Turkish	1	News Paper
392	Aziz Karaca	Amerika'nın Gülen yüzü somurtuyor	3/26/2008	Yeni Mesaj	Turkish	1	News Paper
393	Aziz Karaca	Şu "Türkçe öğretiyoruz" meselesi…	4/29/2008	Yeni Mesaj	Turkish	1	News Paper
394	Aziz Karaca	Savunuyor mu, savuruyor mu?	5/8/2008	Yeni Mesaj	Turkish	1	News Paper
395	Aziz Karaca	Sayın Gülerce güldürmeye de- vam ediyor	5/10/2008	Yeni Mesaj	Turkish	1	News Paper

	Author	Title	Date	Publisher	Language	Gülen	Type
396	Aziz Karaca	"Hizmete" hudut çizilmiyor Mihriban	5/15/2008	Yeni Mesaj	Turkish	1	News Paper
397	Aziz Karaca	Zaman'da Zamanvari bir zamane haberi	5/22/2008	Yeni Mesaj	Turkish	1	News Paper
398	Aziz Karaca	"Ben hizmete hizmet demem, Hizmet bana olmadıkça"	5/29/2008	Yeni Mesaj	Turkish	1	News Paper
399	Aziz Karaca	"ABD dünyaya lazım imiş" Bu-nun için mi?	6/5/2008	Yeni Mesaj	Turkish	1	News Paper
400	Aziz Karaca	Kendi oklarıyla vurulan millet	7/8/2008	Yeni Mesaj	Turkish	1	News Paper
401	Aziz Karaca	KİM: Kitleleri İfsat Merkezi	7/20/2008	Yeni Mesaj	Turkish	1	News Paper
402	Aziz Karaca	BOP'un hizmetinde olanlar Ve "hizmet" adlı yalanlar	10/26/2008	Yeni Mesaj	Turkish	1	News Paper
403	Aziz Karaca	Kiralık gözler, Sam amcadan gözlükler ve…	10/28/2008	Yeni Mesaj	Turkish	1	News Paper
404	Aziz Karaca	Amerika'ya asa Gazi'ye isyan	11/6/2008	Yeni Mesaj	Turkish	1	News Paper

	Author	Title	Date	Publisher	Language	Gülen	Type
405	Aziz Karaca	Paspas gazetesinde paspas olan fikirler	11/9/2008	Yeni Mesaj	Turkish	1	News Paper
406	Aziz Karaca	Kutsal zannederek öptüğüm elin, Ellerime kiri çıktı neyleyim	12/1/2008	Yeni Mesaj	Turkish	1	News Paper
407	Aziz Karaca	Kan gölünde yüzen yüzsüzler	1/8/2009	Yeni Mesaj	Turkish	1	News Paper
408	Aziz Karaca	İhanetin Türkçesi	5/6/2009	Yeni Mesaj	Turkish	1	News Paper
409	Aziz Karaca	Bu kargayı kim besledi?	8/26/2009	Yeni Mesaj	Turkish	1	News Paper
410	Aziz Karaca	Kaleminde bir sızıntı var	8/28/2009	Yeni Mesaj	Turkish	1	News Paper
411	Aziz Karaca	Bedi bereketi var mı kazancın, Çift aboneli hacım	9/9/2009	Yeni Mesaj	Turkish	1	News Paper
412	Aziz Karaca	Hezimet bize hizmet dışarıya	10/16/2009	Yeni Mesaj	Turkish	1	News Paper
413	Aziz Karaca	Bilumum Amerikan uşaklarına…	10/24/2009	Yeni Mesaj	Turkish	1	News Paper

Author	Title	Date	Publisher	Language	Gülen	Type
414 Aziz Karaca	Tesadüfler zinciri !..	10/26/2009	Yeni Mesaj	Turkish	1	News Paper
415 Aziz Karaca	Peçeteyle tutulacak gazeteler	11/7/2009	Yeni Mesaj	Turkish	1	News Paper
416 Aziz Karaca	Amerikancı ekolün okulu	11/8/2009	Yeni Mesaj	Turkish	1	News Paper
417 Aziz Karaca	Fitne Üretim Merkezleri: FÜM	1/30/2010	Yeni Mesaj	Turkish	1	News Paper
418 Aziz Karaca	Irak'ta bir kuş ölse…	4/9/2010	Yeni Mesaj	Turkish	1	News Paper
419 Aziz Karaca	Ilımlı İslam neymiş anladınız mı?	4/12/2010	Yeni Mesaj	Turkish	1	News Paper
420 Aziz Karaca	Gizlenmiş hezimet "hizmet" içinde	5/22/2010	Yeni Mesaj	Turkish	1	News Paper
421 Aziz Karaca	O cenahta yeni bir şey yok	6/7/2010	Yeni Mesaj	Turkish	1	News Paper
422 Aziz Karaca	Siz nelere "evet" demediniz ki?	7/31/2010	Yeni Mesaj	Turkish	1	News Paper

	Author	Title	Date	Publisher	Language	Gülen	Type
423	Aziz Karaca	Amerikan müftüsünden fetvalar	8/5/2010	Yeni Mesaj	Turkish	1	News Paper
424	Aziz Karaca	Kalkın ve doğrulun mezarımızda	8/9/2010	Yeni Mesaj	Turkish	1	News Paper
425	Aziz Karaca	Ölü soyguncuları	8/19/2010	Yeni Mesaj	Turkish	1	News Paper
426	Aziz Karaca	El cevap: Hayır!	8/22/2010	Yeni Mesaj	Turkish	1	News Paper
427	Aytunc Erkin	Fethullah Gülen, Nurettin Veren'i Aradi: Aramizda Halledelim	28/11/2004	Aydinlik	Turkish	1	Magazine
428	noname	Suikastta MOSSAD- Fethullah Hatti	22/12/2002	Aydinlik	Turkish	1	Magazine
429	Zekeriya Beyaz	AB raporu, ic savas yatirimidir"	7/11/2004	Aydinlik	Turkish	1	Magazine
430	Aytunc Erkin	Fethullah Olum Emrimi Verdi"	21/11/2004	Aydinlik	Turkish	1	Magazine
431	Vural Savas	Ugur Mumcu'nun Olum Fermani	28/1/2007	Aydinlik	Turkish	1	Magazine
432	Dogu Perincek	ABD'nin NATO Ulkelerini Kontrol Orgutu: SuperNATO	11/2/2007	Aydinlik	Turkish	1	Magazine

	Author	Title	Date	Publisher	Language	Gülen	Type
433	Ruhsar Senoglu/Serdar Bolat	Fethullah'in Fetvasi Uygulandi, Hz. Muhammed'l Kelime-l Sehadet'ten Cikardilar!	11/2/2007	Aydinlik	Turkish	1	Magazine
434	Sahin Filiz	Diyalog"un Temeli Isa Mesih Hristiyanligi	11/2/2007	Aydinlik	Turkish	1	Magazine
435	Tansu Akgün	CIA NEDEN FETHULLAH GÜLEN'İ DESTEKLİYOR	3/5/2010	Odatv	Turkish	1	website
436	Dogan Duyar	Fethullah'in Ogretmenlerine Amerikan Pasaportu	1/3/1998	Aydinlik	Turkish	1	Magazine

CPSIA information can be obtained at www.ICGtesting.com
Printed in the USA
BVOW041533260612

293632BV00003B/4/P